Post-war reconstruction
in Central America:
Lessons from El Salvador, Guatemala,
and Nicaragua

Patricia Ardón

Translated and
adapted by
Deborah Eade

An Oxfam Working Paper

This work was first published in Guatemala City in May 1998, on behalf of Oxfam GB, as *La paz y los conflictos en Centroamerica*, © CIDECA (Consejo de Investigaciones para el Desarrollo de Centroamerica).

English text first published by Oxfam GB in 1999
Reprinted by Oxfam GB in 1999

© Oxfam GB 1999

ISBN 0 85598 405 8

A catalogue record for this publication is available from the British Library.

Available from the following agents:
USA: Stylus Publishing LLC, PO Box 605, Herndon, VA 20172-0605, USA
tel: +1 (0)703 661 1581; fax: + 1(0)703 661 1547; email: styluspub@aol.com
Canada: Fernwood Books Ltd, PO Box 9409, Stn. 'A', Halifax, N.S. B3K 5S3, Canada
tel: +1 (0)902 422 3302; fax: +1 (0)902 422 3179; e-mail: fernwood@istar.ca
India: Maya Publishers Pvt Ltd, 113-B, Shapur Jat, New Delhi-110049, India
tel: +91 (0)11 649 4850; fax: +91 (0)11 649 1039; email: surit@del2.vsnl.net.in
K Krishnamurthy, 23 Thanikachalan Road, Madras 600017, India
tel: +91 (0)44 434 4519; fax: +91 (0)44 434 2009; email: ksm@md2.vsnl.net.in
South Africa, Zimbabwe, Botswana, Lesotho, Namibia, Swaziland: David Philip Publishers, PO Box 23408, Claremont 7735, South Africa
tel: +27 (0)21 64 4136; fax: +27(0)21 64 3358; email: dppsales@iafrica.com
Tanzania: Mkuki na Nyota Publishers, PO Box 4246, Dar es Salaam, Tanzania
tel/fax: +255 (0)51 180479, email: mkuki@ud.co.tz
Australia: Bush Books, PO Box 1958, Gosford, NSW 2250, Australia
tel: +61 (0)2 043 233 274; fax: +61 (0)2 092 122 468, email: bushbook@ozemail.com.au

Rest of the world: contact Oxfam Publishing, 274 Banbury Road, Oxford OX2 7DZ, UK.
tel. +44 (0)1865 311 311; fax +44 (0)1865 313 925; email publish@oxfam.org.uk

Typeset in Baskerville

Printed and published by Oxfam GB, 274 Banbury Road, Oxford OX2 7DZ, UK

Oxfam GB is a registered charity, no. 202 918, and is a member of Oxfam International.

Contents

Acknowledgements

I learned a great deal during my years with Oxfam GB, and had many remarkable experiences. I hope also to have made my own contribution. I was privileged to know some extraordinary people; not only did we share many things, we also suffered and laughed together even in the midst of situations that were often difficult and dangerous. But above all, as someone who was and remains part of the process of change for the people of Central America, I have had the chance to learn. My thanks to Oxfam GB, and particularly to the Mexico and Central America regional team, for the patience and support they gave me in preparing this paper.

This work is dedicated to all those who lived through the conflicts in Mexico and Central America, and who still hope for a better future; and especially to those who shared with me their sufferings and their joys. And to Patricia Miller, Adolfo Herrera, Luisa Maria Rivera, Martha Thompson, Pauline Martin, Deborah Eade, Morna MacLeod, and Guadalupe Salinas: for everything we experienced together.

Preface

This study originated as a proposal to reflect on the experience of Oxfam GB [1] in Central America during the 1980s, both to contribute to its 'institutional memory' of working in situations of armed conflict, and to trace the relationship between its previous and current work in the region. Oxfam's wider interest coincided with that of its Central American counterparts [2] in reaching a deeper understanding of conflict-resolution as a basis for their own work. This led to the idea of analysing the formal peace-negotiation processes in the region and seeing how civil-society organisations (CSOs) had participated in them, particularly in Guatemala, El Salvador and Nicaragua.

During the course of undertaking this study, I conducted more than 40 interviews with members of NGOs, popular organisations [3], churches, grassroots organisations, women's groups, and ex-combatants. Sadly, much of this rich material was lost in a burglary. Therefore the study draws heavily on other documents, as well as on my own notes and recollections, and on the limited amount of bibliographic research that I was able to conduct.

It soon became obvious, however, that the terms of reference were too wide and the study proposal over-ambitious. In addition, having long been compelled to respond to events in Central America, I had rather under-estimated the value of 'academic' work (not entirely without reason, given how seldom it is of any practical use). Thus I did not fully appreciate that the problem was not just one of time, but also one of having a sound research methodology. It was also clear that it was not feasible to produce something that would be of equal use to all the interested parties, for even if we share a common purpose, our agendas, priorities, and dynamics are all very different.

As a result, this study draws on various different concerns, not all of which have an obvious connection with each other. I trust, nevertheless, that it serves as a basis upon which to reflect more deeply on issues relating to humanitarian endeavour in situations of armed conflict, such as conflict-resolution, participation, international co-operation and forms of intervention, and the dilemmas associated with the transition from war to peace. All these are central to the work of Oxfam as well as to that of the organisations it supports around the world. More importantly, these issues directly affect the lives of the poor majority in Central America.

But the reality I present is itself part of a history that is in so many ways still fragmented; both at a personal and at an institutional level, since so much experience remains locked in the memories of those with whom we worked during the 1980s. Let us hope that one day, there will be a chance to bring together all these fragments within one institutional memory.

Introduction

Today, conflict and conflict-resolution have become 'buzz words' — not only among international agencies, but also among the local and regional actors who are now facing serious challenges on the difficult road towards transition. Transition to what, of course, remains to be seen. One hopes that it will be a transition towards societies that are just, in which people are free to think and to make a real contribution towards building a new future, unhindered by empty stomachs, by constraints on our right to participate, by repression, or by injustice. On the one hand, it is fascinating to see the way in which a growing number of people and organisations are internalising these issues, and finding ways to interpret and practise them in their lives and their work. On the other, I fear that we may be preoccupied with the topic of conflict-resolution for the wrong reasons — to demonstrate that we are not mired in the past, that we are capable of putting forward realistic proposals, that we are not armchair radicals but know what we are talking about. Most importantly, we talk the language of conflict resolution in order to show that we know what we want to say in relation to international co-operation. If this seems over-anxious, it is because I believe we must always be on our guard to ensure that we are genuinely contributing to those processes of change that both derive from, and support, the people — and not just focus on the needs of institutions.

Like many other parts of the world, Central America has recently emerged from a painful period of its history, though one which was also tremendously creative and constructive even in the face of adversity. Mexico, the 'older sibling' who is on the point of joining the First World, offers a warning against the false idea that the beginning or end of the Cold War between the former super-powers is what defines the beginning or the end of the conflicts in Central America. Ideologies may infuse and influence conflicts, but they do not determine them: in Central America, these conflicts are linked to the lack of access to resources, to participation, to creative channels for people's frustrations, to technologies, and to the basic standard of living that every citizen of the world should enjoy, as we stand on the threshold of the 21st century.

But with globalisation, those who are already marginalised will become even less visible, and have even less access to the resources that they need. In other words, what is taking place is the very opposite of what experience tells us needs to happen. Unless, perhaps, this trend makes sense to those who are willing to let the weakest go to the wall? Or, rather, who want to 'stabilise' the trend, given that without the 'small' people, the big ones cannot survive? If stability and the absence of war have become a mechanism by which the world's poor are reduced to becoming the slaves of the rich few, then we non-government organisations (NGOs) must ask ourselves very seriously what our role is: are we working to change the situation of people living in poverty and suffering as a result of conflict – or are we merely alleviating the worst of their pain without addressing its causes? We must therefore ask ourselves why, and how, we should help to resolve conflicts.

International co-operation played an important part in supporting Central American NGOs, popular organisations, and grassroots groups, both during the wars and during the peace processes. One of the harshest criticisms today, however, is of the agencies' lack of analysis of the implications and problems associated with the transition from armed conflict to peace-building. Many Central Americans believe that international aid agencies are today developing their strategies on the basis of their own assumptions, rather than on the capacities of those concerned, or on what is really achievable.

None of the negotiation processes in Central America could have proceeded until the root causes were recognised as lying in the unequal power structures characterising the region, and the chronic and comprehensive exclusion of the poor from participating in shaping their societies. However, as this paper will show, the formal processes (all of which were conducted in a highly secretive manner) responded more to external pressure for stabilisation than to qualitative changes in the underlying causes. Civil-society organisations did gain the chance to participate in political life, and to put forward their own proposals. However, the various accords failed to address the economic, social, and structural problems in any depth. On the contrary, the neo-liberal economic model will tend to deepen the gulf between the rich and the poor, and deprive most people of access to basic services. Increasing poverty and the failure to comply with certain accords is already generating conflicts, and these are in turn impeding the reconstruction of the material infrastructure and of the social fabric which the wars destroyed. In addition, repression and war have left significant psycho-social scars. Women, children, and ex-combatants face particular difficulty in channelling their problems — problems which go beyond individual experiences alone, and affect entire communities and societies.

The opening chapter of this paper reflects on the nature of conflict and identifies various approaches to conflict-resolution and peace-building. In Central America, most of the conflict-resolution efforts were focused on key actors or on the formal leadership structures. Experience shows, however, that the greatest capacity to facilitate peace-building processes is at the middle or intermediary level, if there is sufficient trust and mutual respect among the various parties. Chapter two outlines the peace-negotiation processes in Nicaragua, El Salvador, and Guatemala, focusing on how different sectors of society participated in, or were excluded from, these. Chapter three explores the role of international co-operation in prolonged political and armed conflicts such as those in Central America. The final chapter analyses the insights gleaned from various interlocutors in the region and draws out some general conclusions on the role of international aid agencies both during a period of armed conflict, and in the post-conflict phase.

Chapter One: The importance of analysing conflicts and peace-building processes

International co-operation and conflict

Governments, multilateral agencies (MLAs), donors, and various international events have all helped to make conflict and conflict-resolution a major concern in many parts of the world. This interest has been stimulated both by the need to find new ways of approaching conflict, and by the need of various organisations to re-define their roles and structures in the face of contemporary conflicts in a post-cold war world. The role of the United Nations (UN) is particularly affected by processes of internal restructuring and reviews of working methods.

Why has the theme become so important at the present time? It is not because the number of major armed conflicts has increased — although, if we include 'minor' armed conflicts (defined as those in which at least 25 people are killed in any one year and in which the state is one of the warring parties), there was a rise from 13 in 1989 to 22 in 1992.[4] But the increase in the level of general violence world-wide is not mirrored by a rising incidence of major armed conflicts involving entire populations.

Setting these facts about violence and armed conflict against the widespread perception of a significant rise in armed conflicts, we must take into account the massive changes in information technology over the same period. We can now be swiftly informed not only about the eruption of armed conflict anywhere in the world, but also witness its crudest expression and effects. This may well shape our view of the number and nature of today's armed conflicts, compared with those in years gone by. Moreover, several factors determine what we get to know about a given conflict. Apart from the commercial media interests, which define the importance of information on the basis of whether it is 'topical' or 'spectacular', there are political interests at stake which can ensure that a curtain of silence is drawn over a major conflict. Further, international coverage of armed conflicts is often biased because of the risks faced by reporters and journalists in situations where their safety and ability to function professionally are not guaranteed.

The result is that we fall into the trap of assuming that no news means no conflicts, and become victims of disinformation. Such factors played a role in the Central American conflicts of the 1980s, and particularly in the case of Guatemala, where they resulted in a lack of information about what was happening not only internationally, but also within the country itself.

During the cold war, many armed conflicts in the South were seen (and treated) by most Northern governments and MLAs in ideological terms. Relatively little attention was paid to the underlying structural conditions (for example, patterns of economic or cultural marginalisation), although these were central both to the cause and to the possible resolution of these conflicts in the long term. Instead, armed conflict tended to be seen as a form of confrontation between the super-powers, reflecting the ideological differences at the 'centre', played out on the territory of their Southern 'satellites'.

Between 1989 and 1992, however, some 82 armed conflicts were registered in 60 locations around the world.[5] Most of these occurred in areas where the majority of the population were economically vulnerable, with little access to political power, and precious little access to any form of social service. Ideology was used to explain the existence of most of these conflicts, and in turn influenced the ways in which the warring parties behaved. It also served to justify the massive arms industry in the North. During the cold war, five Northern countries supplied 95 per cent of arms exported to the so-called Third World.[6]

The false understanding of the nature of so many conflicts also translated into mechanisms and approaches to diplomatic relations that have since become redundant. This, along with the serious criticisms of the UN and other agencies over their handling, for example, of emergencies in Somalia and Rwanda, underlines the need to redefine our understanding of the nature of contemporary conflicts, and to re-conceptualise conflict-resolution. The very complexity of modern conflict calls for an analysis that will enable us to understand and engage with the multiple causes of the growing number of internal conflicts, including their often religious and ethnic dimensions.

The absorption of an increasing proportion of official development assistance (ODA) by conflict-related emergencies is also a matter of concern. Clearly, the reduction or re-orientation of the resources available for international co-operation affects those intended to benefit from it, especially since the financial aid necessary to support post-conflict reconstruction is being diverted to new emergencies. But development assistance is (or should be) part of a strategy to reduce the incidence of emergencies, especially in the context of the widening gap between rich and poor, which itself constitutes a risk of renewed outbreaks of conflict. (In 1960, the income of the richest 20 per cent of the world's population was 30 times higher than that of the poorest 20 per cent. By 1990, this gap had doubled, and is still widening.)

Some analysts argue that ODA has now effectively become a new way of managing conflict, given the failure of traditional diplomatic approaches to mediate or resolve such crises. In a post-cold war context of globalisation, the language of 'convergence' is giving way to that of cultural pluralism, which in many cases has brought with it with cultural, ethnic, or political exclusion. In other words, those who hold the greatest concentration of resources and power can no longer rely on an ideological framework that explained all conflicts in terms of East versus West. Instead, they are seeking an explanation in terms of culture. The structural dimensions of conflict are increasingly ignored, as it is easier to explain conflicts in cultural terms, rather than as an outcome of North-South contradictions, or of unequal access to resources or political exclusion within countries.

Given their close involvement in situations of conflict, NGOs have the potential to present an alternative view of its causes and how to resolve them. However, most NGOs lack the capacity to engage in sustained analysis, and even this limited capacity is subject to pressure from funders to demonstrate impact and efficiency, in competing for the ever-dwindling resources available for post-war reconstruction and development. This all too easily leads to situations in which NGOs have a highly influential role within conflict settings, but lack direction due to the absence of analysis and strategic thinking. These deficiencies also mean that NGOs may fail to take into account the real needs arising from the transition from war to peace-building, a risk which is heightened by their need to demonstrate short-term impact.

This has become a critical issue in Central America, because many of the NGOs which, while the revolutionary movements were active, believed in the possibility of structural transformation, now find themselves having to adapt their policies to the reality of globalisation and the new international political order. But many are doing so without sharing responsibility with local counterpart organisations, which will face the challenges of transition in the long term.

Conflict theories

A fashionable theme, conflict has become the subject of many studies and different approaches. There is growing concern that it is vital, before intervening in a conflict, to understand its many contributory factors. The various theories and concepts of conflict provide useful analytical tools, some of which offer valuable insights into approaches to conflict-resolution.

The British NGO Responding to Conflict identifies three main schools of thought.

Power. This describes an ancient theory which holds that human beings and social groups are intrinsically engaged in a power struggle, and seek to dominate others. The term 'balance of power' refers to the minimum force required to ensure coexistence.

Structuralism. This approach looks at the various social institutions and structures which are based on exploitation and therefore generate conflict. It holds that people become trapped in certain structures, in which there are winners and losers.

Liberal pluralism. This considers the fact that human beings become involved in conflicts on a range of levels, in which concepts of 'human needs', communication, and perception are important. Efforts to co-operate may, therefore, either alleviate or aggravate a given situation.

Wehr (1979) described seven different theories of conflict, although he generally recognises that real conflicts are the result of many inter-linking and interdependent factors:

1. Conflict and aggressiveness are innate in all social animals, including human beings, and are part of their biological make-up.

2. Social conflict originates in certain social forms, and in the ways in which societies are structured (for example, where control is imposed by some classes or groups over others).

3. Conflict is a deviation from what is normal, usual, or expected behaviour.

4. Conflicts arise because they serve to strengthen social systems (for example, by reinforcing certain social relations or by relieving social pressure through conflict).

5. Societal conflict arises because the nation-state has national interests that are mutually incompatible (for instance, in relation to security, power, and prestige).

6. Conflict is the result of a breakdown of communication, of false perceptions, of socialisation, and other psychological processes of which we are largely unaware — a view which holds that conflict is based on perceptions rather than on material realities.

7. Conflict is a natural process common to all societies, and is somewhat predictable. Thus, it can be handled in a constructive and non-violent way.

The last of these theories — that conflict can be handled constructively and non-violently — underpins most thinking and practice in the field of conflict-resolution.

What do we mean by conflict and conflict-resolution?

Conflicts manifest themselves on many levels, individual and collective, personal as well as public: therein lies their diversity. Conflict is a part of life itself, and is expressed in our everyday activities. Thus, it is an integral and dialectical feature of individual and social dynamics. If handled appropriately, it can give rise to creative ways to bring about change; otherwise it remains a destructive force.

We see conflict as a dynamic and changing process that is rooted in various structures (in social, economic, political, gender-related and other aspects of identity). However, it may also be aggravated, 're-cycled', or sustained on the basis of either mutual perceptions or accumulated hatreds and hostilities. This may happen over a prolonged period, or in contexts in which the conflicting parties have been involved in violent confrontation, with the consequent costs in terms of human life, and material and emotional well-being. Thus, conflict-resolution is intimately linked to peace-building through processes which address the multi-layered complexity of conflict.

Here, I refer principally to armed conflicts with a nationwide dimension, which are collective and organised in character. At the same time, we see the dynamic of conflict as a historical 'continuum' – a dynamic which precedes armed hostilities and usually survives the formal peace negotiations in some form.

Concepts of conflict-resolution

It is important at this point to define how I use some of the concepts adopted in this paper, many of which are now common currency among MLAs, NGOs, and other organisations.

Sustainable peace. This is a peace based on a solid agreement, with certain guarantees of irreversibility, in a dynamic post-war period. The various stages in building such a peace are not necessarily sequential in terms of time; they range from the emergency phase through to efforts to consolidate the possibility of development, from disarmament and detente to the building of harmonious and consensus-based social relations. The term implies efforts to build a society in which every citizen has access to resources and to power.

Peace is a complex social construct, a fabric woven with the many threads that make up a society, such as the material, cultural, psycho-symbolic, and political dimension. Thus, working for sustainable peace entails focusing on the immediate goals, while also maintaining a medium- and long-term perspective.

Civil society. This term refers to all institutions and groups that are not part of the formal structures of the state. However, this paper focuses on the organised participation of the poor majority in shaping the society they live in. In this way, the term 'civil society' allows us to understand how, and in which circumstances, processes within a society affects its political processes. This contrasts with approaches which look exclusively at the state, political parties, and social élites. It also contrasts with those approaches which only consider social movements (Pearce 1996).

Reconciliation. This approach must concentrate on the construction or reconstruction of new relations between previously antagonistic individuals or social groups. It involves not only the tangible aspects, but also the emotional and psychological dimensions of the conflict, in order to deal with the past and to identify new forms of coexistence and future inter-relationships. According to Lederach (Lederach 1994), the basic aim of reconciliation is to seek new 'spaces' among the affected population, where they can confront and assimilate the painful past and the necessarily shared future, as a means of addressing the present.

Participation. This process creates the conditions for every sector of society (particularly those hitherto excluded) to exercise decision-making power, by formulating policies and shaping actions that affect them and their country.

It is also useful to define certain roles in the processes of negotiating peace and resolving conflict:

Mediation. Mediation can take place over a limited period, or it can be part of a long-term process to identify any points of agreement between the parties involved in the conflict, in order to achieve a common goal. Mediators analyse, interpret, and identify points of agreement in such a way as to facilitate dialogue between the adversaries, and sometimes to develop specific proposals for each to consider.

Monitoring. By following up the process and the observance of a peace accord or agreement, monitoring is a means to ensure that the former adversaries are aware of progress made, or of the reasons for non-fulfilment.

Facilitation. This term covers a wide range of functions in enabling adversaries to meet, such as assisting the various parties to come together, providing the necessary time and space, interpreting the parties' aims to each other, and so on.

Moderation. Individuals or groups moderating conflict resolution must ensure that the fighting parties enjoy equal opportunities to make known their positions, and that the process is conducted in conditions favourable to dialogue and negotiation.

What do we mean by peace-building?

Lederach considers that peace-building essentially represents the challenge of creating and sustaining transformed social relations in a movement towards a peace that is thus sustainable. The dynamic nature both of conflicts and of efforts to resolve them requires us to analyse the many contributory factors, which interact in generating and transforming them. Peace-building also implies the interaction of diverse national and international actors, in a process which involves a whole range of approaches and actions needed to transform the conflict into relationships and results that are both sustainable and peaceful (Lederach, op.cit.).

Thus, peace-building is not merely the concrete outcome of a formal negotiation process or cease-fire but also implies the building of a social dynamic, which requires social transformation in order to sustain it. In other words, it is a *process of building and sustaining peace*. This process requires us to address both the substantive problems underlying the conflict, and the dynamics of *relations* and *perceptions* that evolve throughout such conflicts, and which (as noted above) may be 're-cycled' and perpetuated.

Conflict-resolution must be based on a recognition of the need for, and the wish to seek, peaceful solutions. It must be a deliberate effort to know and understand the other's logic, not in order to surrender to it, but rather in order to identify and proceed on the basis of those points of agreement which may exist in spite of past perceptions. This also means identifying those problems and dynamics where there are no such points of agreement, so that a resolution may be sought in the context of a shared vision of the future.

This represents an enormous challenge, especially in the case of prolonged conflicts. It requires all parties to change their mind-set in relation to the violence, and the negative perceptions that armed conflict generates. Conflict-resolution must work within the context of power relations which are highly resistant to change, and which will ultimately determine whether a sustainable peace can be achieved. Often, there is a 'natural' resistance to change, simply because it is easier to deal with what is familiar. Change is a highly complex matter for anyone who has been directly involved in armed conflict: it calls into question an identity that has been constructed or reinforced within the framework of war, an identity which provides a certain security among those who share its logic. Building a different attitude thus demands change and transformation in an individual's emotional and cultural identity, as well as in those structures and dynamics which govern social and political relations, and access to power and resources.

Clearly, such a comprehensive process also depends on dedicated human resources, both short-term and permanent. Apart from the formal negotiation processes, experience in Central America shows how important it is to draw on individuals who not only understand the problem, but whose credibility and legitimacy allows them to be a real resource in the longer term. It is equally important to establish meeting spaces (both actual locations and symbolic opportunities for expression) and groups where, and among which, debates, experimentation, and change can flourish.

The complexity of transition

Transition from armed conflict to peace is necessarily complex, and usually full of ambiguities. One major problem in formal peace negotiations is that people's expectations are so high that the process can seem extremely slow, while at the same time events may move more quickly than people can easily handle. It is not unusual for parties to feel that a great deal has been given away in return for very little, while the rapid pace at which the process evolves can make it hard for ordinary people to participate.

A central but largely overlooked issue is that of identity. In war-time, one's identity is often defined in opposition to that of the enemy. People form very strong group identities, and tend to cling to what is familiar, even when change might actually benefit them. In addition, the ambiguities of a transition period, and the lack of a setting in which people can feel a sense of security and belonging, pose enormous challenges. The situation facing ex-combatants is particularly difficult: their identity as fighters is not merely questioned, but actually wiped out in the post-conflict period. (In addition, they have to deal with the emotional effects of having fought in the conflict.)

Open warfare or acute conflict imposes certain ground-rules. People's very survival depends whose side they are on, whether or not they are directly involved in the fighting. The peace-building process depends on people being able to form new alliances. People naturally fear that they will be co-opted, so it is hard for them to be open to new ideas or discussions. Such fears are not merely subjective, nor will they automatically be resolved in the process of establishing a 'culture of peace'. Paradoxically, the strong feelings of belonging, of a secure identity, which people often develop as a response to the real conditions of the war, may translate into violent behaviour once those conditions are no longer present.

Peace-negotiation processes must lead to genuine changes in the situations that initially gave rise to the conflicts, but this may pose a dilemma. In Central America, it was not only poverty that sparked off the conflicts, but also the exclusion of the vast majority of citizens from any real participation in the decisions affecting their country. Of course, some social groups will try to maintain the status quo at all costs. Thus, peace-building has to challenge the structural underpinning of the status quo, as well as the daily exercise of power, in order that this become a force for social transformation, for peaceful-co-existence, and part of the process of establishing new social relations between individuals, and among groups.

Often, large elements of the population have never experienced *the positive (active) exercise of power*. They have been unable to choose and to do as they please, because in times of acute conflict, there is merely the power to protect oneself and to survive (the negative exercise of power). The positive exercise of power depends on people's capacity to transform both themselves and the world around them. Peace-building, therefore, entails strengthening this capacity, or *empowering* the marginalised, so that they can become protagonists in the process.

This long-term view of transition does not merely look at the passage of time between war and peace, but also implies (re)training individuals in activities unconnected to the war; enabling people to reclaim their human dignity; seeing the past as a tool with which to rebuild the present and the future; and making the society as a whole aware of how deeply some of its members have suffered as a result of the war. It includes attending to the specific needs of ex-combatants, of women, and of children. These are just a few of the factors that help a society not only to come to terms with what it has lived through, and enable each individual to recognise that she or he has a vital role to play in building something new.

The issue of psycho-social trauma also needs to be addressed, not only for the main protagonists, but also for those who suffered the impact of the conflict. People throughout Central America, and in Guatemala in particular, have lived through intensely painful experiences: the loss of human life and of material possessions, constant and widespread violence, torture, repression, rape, abuse, and discrimination. The long-term consequences of such traumatic experiences can scarcely be imagined.

Thus, building a sustainable peace starts in the context of a transition which may be vague in direction or not based on a broad social consensus — a transition towards what? It must work simultaneously on several levels (technical and political) and at different paces (immediate and longer-term), while also responding to people's diverse needs and capacities, and addressing the expressions of conflict both at the structural level and in everday life. Indeed, some analysts (Lederach 1994, Galtung 1995) argue that people and their social relations are the real vehicle for transition and are just as important as the either the technical or the underlying concerns. This contrasts with the conventional top-down approach to negotiation and conflict-resolution, which tends to ignore the many actors and layers of social relations which will in the long run determine to what extent the peace will be sustainable. Formal negotiation is only one element in peace-building. It tends to emphasise the need for changes in the combatants' behaviour, either because of the cessation of hostilities is a precondition for progress, or because it is clear that the war will not have a decisive outcome. Because of this narrow range of motivations, the need for change within society as a whole is often disregarded.

A society emerging from armed conflict will naturally expect that the negotiations will also provide a long-term solution to its problems, whereas the international community may measure the success of the negotiation process

simply in terms of a non-return to war. This makes it all the more important to invest in other social processes which can take forward the kinds of changes necessary to guarantee a lasting peace.

Negotiation

If we have in mind a more integrated vision of peace-building, then we must encourage processes which will bring together people from across the social spectrum, at all different levels, but with a sense of shared responsibility. Such a vision would mean letting go of the notion that anyone has a monopoly on the truth, since genuine dialogue cannot take place without doing so. The creativity thus released would enable us to move away from traditional patterns of thought, while at the same time grounding ourselves in reality, and seeing all the elements that contribute to conflict. Rather than concentrating solely on the leaders, we would come to see the full participation of people from the grassroots and intermediate levels of society as critical to achieving peace. The inter-related nature of all these elements is illustrated in the following diagram prepared by the NGO, Responding to Conflict:

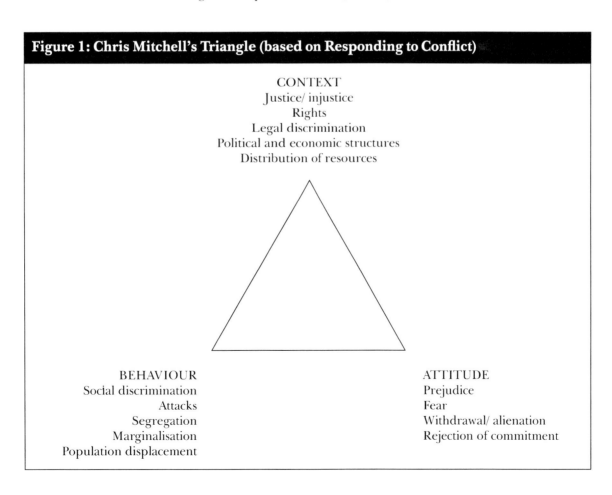

Figure 1: Chris Mitchell's Triangle (based on Responding to Conflict)

CONTEXT
Justice/ injustice
Rights
Legal discrimination
Political and economic structures
Distribution of resources

BEHAVIOUR
Social discrimination
Attacks
Segregation
Marginalisation
Population displacement

ATTITUDE
Prejudice
Fear
Withdrawal/ alienation
Rejection of commitment

This triangle shows how important it is to focus not only on the material aspects of any given context, but also on the social dimensions, such as discrimination and lack of access to decision-making fora, which in turn generate attitudes that must change in order to achieve broad-based participation. Equally important are the various perceptions of reality, since these often govern the behaviour and attitudes of individuals and groups towards the 'enemy'. To take all these factors into account means, as we have said, combining short-term actions with an awareness of the wider political, economic, social, psychological, and cultural dimensions; and at the same time developing a clear vision of what would constitute a desirable future.

I have already noted that formal peace processes tend to proceed in a hierarchical rather than an organic fashion. The importance of involving those sectors which are not part of the political elite, so that the process is widely 'owned', is often ignored. It is also vital to look critically at how far the assumed leaders are truly representative of and in full dialogue with people at the grassroots. It is often assumed, wrongly, that the views of leaders will automatically be adopted by those they represent. Such leaders may come to symbolise wider hopes, but prove unable to respond to people's more immediate needs. They may be obliged to assume a public or official role which places certain constraints upon them. They may be under pressure to bow to the 'strategic need' to bring about an end to the armed conflict, especially if this has been very prolonged. Such factors can make it hard for these leaders to maintain close contact with people at the grassroots. In some cases, they may even feel a greater need than before for their own personal and private space.

So the political élite cannot determine whether or not society will feel the need to get involved in the peace process, or that it will develop the necessary skills to do so. In El Salvador and Guatemala, for instance, where the peace negotiations went on almost in secret, it became extremely difficult to ensure any form of communication between the leaders involved and the population. This is one reason why it is so important to have individuals and groups acting as facilitators and developing plans of action. Irrespective of whether they will themselves ultimately benefit from the process, such people are invaluable resources in encouraging new social relations.

While such individuals are likely to have established their personal legitimacy in relation to the conflict and the various actors involved, they also need institutional backing. This combination has proven a key factor in enabling such 'resource people' to mediate or facilitate in conflict-resolution. A good example is that of an international NGO in El Salvador which lent its reputation, and that of certain individual staff-members, to efforts to establish a dialogue and eventually reach a consensus between the opposing parties. Similarly, in the Atlantic Coast of Nicaragua, the Moravian Church played a crucial role in achieving peaceful outcomes to the armed conflict. Obviously, such efforts are enhanced when the various individuals and institutions know and are willing to co-operate with each other.

Conclusion: From conflict to peace

Conflict-resolution efforts must, therefore, be based on approaches which address the strategic dimensions of the problems, and the objectives that each side views as important, not merely on the conceptual differences. The methods and tools employed should aim to empower those social actors with least access to power and resources, while also helping them to see the potential for a peaceful solution to their problems, and equipping them with specific skills such as negotiating and lobbying techniques.

The basic dilemma is how to create a form of peace which can transform the negative conditions that gave rise to, or perpetuated, the conflict into positive forces with which to build something new. Such transformation does not happen in a vacuum, but in a context riddled with contradictions, and one in which many actors do not participate actively. The task is thus to transform society, and to build new ways of relating to each other and of handling power which are based on inclusion, rather than exclusion, and which can guarantee the fullest possible participation.

Finally, it is important to be aware of the various agendas at play in peace-building and conflict-resolution. Methodologies may show us how to handle conflict, but not necessarily how to resolve it. Similarly, no one system is in itself the answer: finding a way to deal with the many complex issues at stake can only be based on what the people involved actually want — particularly those who are relatively powerful. This can only happen if all social sectors participate.

Chapter Two: The peace negotiation processes in Central America

A brief overview of the political background to the conflict situations in Nicaragua, El Salvador, and Guatemala is followed by accounts of the negotiation processes and peace accords in each of these countries.

Background

The 1980s saw the fiercest conflict in the region this century, with enormous costs in terms of loss of life, infrastructure, human development, and psycho-social well-being. Although the warring parties in each country discussed here have signed peace accords (Guatemala was the last to do so in December 1996), peace as such, as well as the democratisation processes, are still fragile. In the context of economic globalisation, it is unlikely that the conflicts will disappear altogether, especially given the ever-diminishing opportunities for most Central Americans to attain a reasonable standard of living. That said, it is also clear that new political openings in the region may allow for peaceful solutions to the crises facing it.

For centuries, Central America has oscillated between armed conflict on the one hand, and efforts to harmonise and integrate the region, on the other. This background becomes even more relevant in the face of globalisation, because opportunities for economic advancement are seriously limited by the region's unequal relations with industrialised nations. As Central America seeks to compete in the international market, this in turn generates greater inequalities within each country. Both the conflicts and efforts to create a regional identity (at least at the economic level) are rooted in history. In the 1950s, various intra-regional projects aimed to establish regional unity through economic integration. In the 1960s, the Central American Common Market was quite successful. However, these attempts have been repeatedly thwarted by the cycles of internal conflict, and by the competition among neighbouring countries to gain access to international markets.

The process of 'pacification' was part of a series of initiatives put forward from the 1970s by major regional and external actors. The role played by the USA deserves special mention, because the nature of its intervention in the region turned it into one of the main actors.

The 1979 Nicaraguan revolution, which brought to power the Sandinista liberation movement had a major impact on Central America. The US Administration embarked on an undeclared war against the Sandinista government, significantly increasing its direct political and military intervention in the Salvadoran conflict from bases in Honduras, as well as its provision of military advice and intelligence to Guatemala. Within Latin America, some countries defended the position of the US, but most expressed concern that the 'internationalisation' of the conflict might endanger the peace and security of the entire continent.

Against this backdrop, in January 1983 the governments of Colombia, Mexico, Panama, and Venezuela formed the Contadora Group. (In 1985, other Latin American countries formed a Contadora support group, known as the Lima Group.) Contadora's aim was to achieve peace in Central America by holding free elections and ensuring respect for social, political, and civil rights, particularly in Nicaragua and El Salvador. These initiatives, and particularly the Contadora process, contributed to a favourable climate for peace following the first meeting of the warring parties in Esquipulas, Guatemala, on 25 May 1986. On 7 August 1987, the presidents of the region signed a peace accord, known as Esquipulas II. This accord was based on the peace plan proposed by President Oscar Arias of Costa Rica, which drew on certain elements from the Contadora initiative but also sought to bring about peace and reconciliation through a process of national dialogue. Esquipulas II thus provided the 'means for establishing firm and lasting peace' — but without interference from various external actors which had previously tried to mediate in the regional conflict. For the first time, it created an instrument that acknowledged the internal roots of the conflicts (as opposed to an analysis which saw them in terms of a cold-war confrontation), that focused on the region's own development problems, and that highlighted the urgent need for international economic aid, particularly in relation to foreign debt.

The Esquipulas II negotiations also introduced concepts and mechanisms which represented a qualitative leap forward, through establishing communication among the region's governments, and by generating the trust necessary for the various actors to enter into dialogue with each other. Building on what had been developed through the Contadora Group, Esquipulas II included a timetable for meeting and evaluating each party's commitments; the so-called 'symmetrical' definition of the causes of the crisis (which meant that they were no longer seen as based only in one country, or reduced to one focal point); and the agreement that implementation would be simultaneous throughout the region, which helped to reduce the levels of mistrust among the parties concerned. At the same time, a presidential summit ensured that these matters would be dealt with at the highest decision-making level.

The 1987 Esquipulas II peace accord opened the way for negotiated settlements. It also demonstrated that the specific mechanisms for peace must be accepted unanimously throughout the region, and based on consensus among each of the national governments. It also underlined the need for national reconciliation, stressing that dialogue should be the main instrument to promote '... actions directed at national reconciliation that allowed for popular participation, and exercise of civil and political rights on the part of the citizens of Central America'.

However, the negotiations did not yield fruit immediately. In Guatemala, little progress was made between the Guatemalan National Revolutionary Unit (URNG) and Vinicio Cerezo's Christian Democrat government. In El Salvador, the dialogue between the government and the Democratic Revolutionary Front/ Farabundo Martí Liberation Front (FDR-FMLN) stalled after the president of the non-government Human Rights Commission was murdered. In Nicaragua, the government unexpectedly decided to hold direct discussions with the right-wing *contra* leaders, and agreed a partial cease-fire. This caused profound rifts within the *contra* leadership, raising major questions about the role of the US government. The Honduran government's continued denial of the presence of permanent *contra* bases on its territory, even though their existence was public

knowledge, was the source of growing tensions in the border area.

The Esquipulas II accord was a futher step in establishing mechanisms to guarantee the political democratisation process, setting dialogue and verification as the starting points for reconciliation. It was assumed that this would incorporate all sectors of civil society. As described below, this process took on different characteristics in each country.

Extraordinary events took place during 1989–90: the FMLN offensive in El Salvador in November 1989 demonstrated that it had not been defeated militarily; the US invaded Panama in December 1989; in February 1990, elections in Nicaragua ushered in a centre-right coalition; right-wing governments were returned to power in elections in Costa Rica and Honduras; the UN initiated a mediation process in El Salvador; and the URNG and various political parties and others began discussions in Guatemala. All this contributed to a new regional dynamic and made peace seem achievable. A major factor was the electoral defeat of the FSLN in Nicaragua, which greatly altered US policy towards the region. With the disappearance of the supposed Communist threat in Nicaragua, Costa Rica and Honduras ceased to be favoured recipients of US economic aid.

At the same time, amnesty laws opened up the space for dialogue with the opposition forces in each country, provided these disarmed. (This was part of the Esquipulas accord: paragraph 15 of the 1989 Costa del Sol Declaration made the first call for all irregular forces throughout the region to disarm.) In terms of the participation of civil-society groups in the peace processes, Esquipulas II called for the establishment of National Reconciliation Commissions, in order '... to verify adherence to the commitments undertaken by the five Central American governments in signing this document with regard to amnesty, cease-fire, democratisation and free elections ... and to monitor the national reconciliation process, as well as the unrestricted respect and full guarantees for all citizens within any genuinely democratic political processes'.

The events of the late 1980s thus marked a new phase in the regional conflict. This period also saw a grave deterioration in the living conditions of the vast majority of Central Americans. The acute economic crisis could no longer be ignored — nor could the role of US economic aid, which had been critical during the armed conflicts, especially in El Salvador and Nicaragua. Between 1980 and 1990, the US government had increased its bilateral aid from US$185 million to US$1,092 million. The dependence on trade with the USA also increased dramatically, and remittances from family members in the USA had become an important element of the region's economies, particularly of El Salvador's. However, although the presidents of Central America had calculated that some US$10 billion in aid would be needed over the next five years to support the peace processes, the US government cut its bilateral aid by 20 per cent, arguing that trade, not aid, was the answer. This posed a great challenge. In 1970, Central America accounted for about 1.9 per cent of 'Third World' international trade. By 1988, this had fallen to 0.6 per cent, coffee being the only significant product for the world market.

A degree of political stability had begun to emerge, and the UN started to play an important role in the peace processes, from demobilising the *contra* forces, supervising the Esquipulas II accords on intra-regional arms trade, to mediating in the Salvadoran peace talks, and facilitating the dialogue between the URNG and the government of Guatemala. But despite these encouraging signs, most Central Americans still enjoyed very little participation in the political processes, and had little access to ever scarcer resources.

At the end of 1991, the Salvadoran Peace Accords were signed; while in Guatemala, dialogue continued for several years, until the Arzu government and the URNG eventually signed the an accord in December 1996. A fragile peace had also been achieved in Nicaragua, although this was undermined by the unwillingness of certain elements of the *contra* forces to lay down their arms — a problem that lasted until 1997.

Despite the overall achievements of the peace process, even today there are still isolated cases of people resorting to arms in order to resolve political problems. And Central America is immersed in an economic crisis in which the poor are getting poorer, and in which it is ever harder to halt, much less reverse, the increase of violence and social disintegration. Drug trafficking is a major problem, and in some countries involves high-ranking government officials — especially among the military. For many Mexicans and Central Americans, migration to the North remains the only option, given that neither the armed struggle nor the possibility of meaningful political participation offer any real hope of a better life.

NICARAGUA

Background

'Here, our main conflict is grinding poverty.' This wry comment was made by someone from the Northern Autonomous Region of the Nicaraguan Atlantic Coast, and the situation is set to worsen throughout the country. Today, Nicaragua not only faces the same structural problems that confront the region as a whole. Within the process of reconciliation, it also faces great economic and social challenges in the aftermath of a conflict which, in the 1980s alone, killed some 30,000 people and directly affected about 900,000 people. The war caused US$17 billion's worth of damage, and destroyed the farming economy and agricultural productive capacity. It caused profound social divisions and did serious damage to community and family structures, as well as leaving deep emotional and cultural wounds. To make matters worse, in October 1988 Hurricane Joan almost completely destroyed some settlements on the Atlantic Coast, and badly affected production in other areas of the country.

The war in Nicaragua was unusual: the country had already lived through an armed conflict which began in the 1960s, when the FSLN was founded. Their armed struggle against the Somoza dictatorship lasted almost 20 years and ended with the overthrow of the Somoza regime on 19 July 1979. It is important to remember that the burden of fighting to bring down Somoza was carried mainly by the poorer sectors of society. The dictatorship had repressed any form of opposition and presided over a decline in general living standards. The prevailing ideological climate, and the then fashionable concept of political vanguards, gave a somewhat military flavour to the way in which ordinary Nicaraguans participated in the opposition movements. Furthermore, the struggle to overthrow Somoza was rooted mainly in the Spanish-speaking Pacific Coast, where the capital, Managua, is situated. The FSLN simply assumed that the revolutionary process would be understood and shared by indigenous and ethnic minority groups on the Atlantic Coast. However, these groups came from quite distinct cultural backgrounds, and from a geographical area that had historically been marginalised from the country's 'development'. This made the war on the Atlantic Coast very different from the conflicts in the rest of the region, and eventually led to the Regional Autonomy process.

Despite detractors within — but mostly outside — Nicaragua, there is no doubt that during its early years, the Sandinista Government galvanised the desire of most Nicaraguans for a democratic society. There was an unprecedented level of popular organisation and political participation. For instance, during Somoza's dictatorship, there had been only 133 registered unions nationwide, with 27,000 members. After 1979, this number grew to 207,000 members, organised in more than 1,200 trade unions. Organisations of peasant farmers, women, educators, and so on flourished; and the government's mass adult-literacy and health campaigns depended on the voluntary involvement of thousands of Nicaraguan citizens. The Sandinistas believed that popular democracy implied the organisational development of civil society, and wanted to reinforce this by establishing a broad alliance between industrial workers and peasant farmers, within a predominantly rural economy. (The agricultural sector then represented about 50 per cent of the economically active population in Nicaragua.)

Thus, the popular organisations on the Pacific Coast expanded enormously. However, their qualitative development was more modest, because the war had a major impact on their fledgling organisational processes. The conflict thwarted concepts such as popular democracy and affected popular organisations' participation in civil society. In addition, most of the leadership of the most powerful economic sectors, who were opposed to what the Sandinistas represented, had left the country. Thus they did not fully engage in the political debates within Nicaragua until the late 1980s. Indeed, most of the opposition to the Sandinista government was in fact conceived and organised from outside the country. This background not only is key to understanding the economic impact of the war, but also explains the remarkable level of awareness among ordinary Nicaraguans of their political and social rights, and reveals the longer-term repercussions of the conflict in shaping people's identities.

The revolutionary process, and the FSLN government in particular, became the targets in a war of attrition waged by sympathisers of the Somocista regime, and by those who began to question the Sandinistas' policies, especially in relation to land reform, and to the compulsory military service introduced as a result of the war. Throughout the ten years that the FSLN was in power, the armed conflict was fuelled by the US government's unswerving support for the contra forces. Its fiercely anti-communist ideology, which saw everything in cold-war terms, effectively cast Nicaragua as a leading actor in the regional conflict.

Most analysts believe that the 1989 electoral defeat of the FSLN was due largely to the human and social exhaustion caused by the war, to the distancing of the leadership from its own supporters, and to an acute economic crisis arising both from the war and from the US blockade. Today, supporters of both sides and middle-level popular leaders alike are disenchanted with the lack of solutions to their shared problems. These were not resolved by the war and have, if anything, become more complex since then.

At the same time, the disarmament process has been far from perfect. The rapid decline in most Nicaraguans' economic situation has led to an increasing level of social disintegration and a worsening of living conditions, especially among women and children. Although the political conflict continues to be part of national life, the extent to which violence has become simply a way of ensuring physical survival has pushed politics far from the hearts and minds of many Nicaraguans.

The economic crisis can be measured in terms of the unprecedented level of foreign debt — the worst in the Western hemisphere. It can also be seen in the effects of structural adjustment policies, resulting in cuts to government spending which have further limited people's access to public services. In addition, the offers of international co-operation, on which so many hopes had been pinned with the signing of the Accords, have largely failed to materialise. Official aid to the new government of Nicaragua amounted to only US$3 billion between 1990 and 1993, and has been declining since 1991. Of the total received up to 1995, 40 per cent was used to service the foreign debt, and 57 per cent

on imports or specific projects. Only US$11.5 million of the US$614.3 million donated by the US government during this period was earmarked for social programmes. Ironically, the various international allies whose support was so strategic during the war — whether to the Sandinistas or to the National Resistance or *contra* — are now either unable or unwilling to provide assistance.

As for non-government aid, the international agencies have also undergone budget cuts and are under pressure to re-focus their programmes. Those still working in Nicaragua have had to re-define their role in a rapidly changing context, and review their objectives and strategies vis-à-vis their local counterparts and towards the government's neo-liberal policies. Many Nicaraguan NGOs, most of which emerged during the war and were strongly influenced by the state, are now immersed in a transition that calls for capacities and resources that far outstrip their real potential. This has constrained their ability either to make proposals or to respond to demands, in spite of their wealth of innovative experiences in the fields of organisation and production.

The situation is worsened by the culture of dependency which was the outcome both of the war-time state and of the enormous, and unconditional, international financial support given to the Sandinistas during the 1980s – a culture very hard to overcome within a transition process. Paradoxically, most observers agree that Nicaraguans retain a strong awareness of their rights, and a deep desire for peace. These characteristics may constitute their main strength in building alternatives for the future.

The formal post-war reconciliation process

In Nicaragua, the Esquipulas Accord encouraged civil-society organisations to become more involved in the post-war reconciliation process. When, in 1985, the US Administration openly declared its intention to bring down the Sandinista government — intensifying its support for military actions as well as introducing a trade embargo which was to generate the most severe economic crisis in the country's history – it justified its actions by painting the Sandinistas as a dictatorship which supressed all independent associational life. In fact, the Sandinistas had initiated a daring project discussing autonomy for ethnic groups in the Atlantic Coast region as far back as 1984, which showed a remarkable grasp of issues of diversity. Similarly, the 1984 elections — through which the Sandinistas sought to gain national and international legitimacy — sent a clear signal that Nicaraguans had a part to play in the democratic process. The elections were in essence an attempt to put an end to the US-sponsored armed aggression.

In 1988, the Sandinistas participated actively in the Esquipulas II process. They sought to engage politically with their neighbours, in order to consolidate their legitimacy and establish relationships that would at least hold back others from undermining their own efforts to establish a negotiated and lasting peace. In this spirit, the National Reconciliation Commission (CNR) was set up under the leadership of the Catholic church. Local and regional Peace Commissions were also formed, drawing together various civil society representatives, and aiming to facilitate meetings and dialogue between the warring factions. The Nicaraguan opposition also called for national dialogue, seeking to gather support for what would eventually become the electoral alliance known as the National Opposition Union (UNO).

The conflict-resolution process made concrete progress in the August 1989 Tela Summit. This saw the establishment of the 'Joint Plan for the demobilisation and repatriation or voluntary relocation within Nicaragua and third countries of members of the National Resistance (*contra*) and their families ...'. The document set down conditions for the demobilised fighters which were to be supported by various international organisations. Implicit in this was the offer of amnesty to anyone who applied for it.

The Esquipulas II Accords went further still, and included the commitment to hold democratic elections and embark on bilateral negotiations between the Sandinistas and the National Resistance. This marked an effort to take the debate out of the military sphere and into the political arena, and to reintegrate the combatants into civilian life. However, it was the electoral process which defined the end of the war, taking place as it did in the context of a government weakened by the war, the US economic blockade, and externally-supported aggression.

The offer of amnesty was opposed by some high-level Sandinistas as well as by the *contra* leaders. Irrespective of any formal agreements, neither group was psychologically or politically ready to make a transition. However, a growing number of small agreements were gradually

reached between the military leaders of both camps. The Sapoa Agreement had brought them together for the first time, although no advance was made on the demobilisation front, largely because of the political conditions laid down. Some of the military leaders had begun to establish informal (and unofficial) channels of communication even before political agreements had been formalised.

At the same time, there were renewed reconciliation initiatives within civil society. The National Reconciliation Commission was headed by the Catholic hierarchy, but the local Peace Commissions also made concrete efforts to facilitate dialogue and to undertake certain mediation activities. Many of these initiatives were almost spontaneous in character. More often than not, they were based on the support of individuals and groups who were seen to have some authority within the communities and the warring parties, rather than on formal or permanent structures.

The war officially finished two months after the election of the UNO government, with the signing of a cease-fire agreement on 18 April 1990. However, in spite of the official pro-nouncements and meetings, it was not for another eight months, under US pressure, that the *contra* began to demobilise. While the elections were intended to reduce the tensions between the warring parties, they actually intensified polarisation within Nicaragua. The elections had brought to power a very heterogeneous alliance, supported by the US government and led by Violeta Chamorro (a former member of the first Sandinista *junta*, and widow of a renowned journalist who had opposed the Somocista regime). No sooner had the elections been held than a Transition Accord was signed which aimed to ensure an orderly and peaceful transition. This was described both by the left and by the extreme right as a *co-government*, and was to be based on reconciliation at the highest levels. The document itself called for social reconciliation: '... the firm bases must be laid down for reconciliation, national harmony and stability in every sense, in order to create an environment of trust and security for all Nicaraguans ...' (Protocol of the proceedings of the transfer of the presidency of the Republic of Nicaragua, 27 March 1990). However, no firm commitments to provide social assistance or economic opportunities were made, which meant that the Accord offered no security either for working people or for the demobilised fighters.

This policy vacuum contributed to isolated cases of re-armament and also led to widespread strikes between April and November 1990 which endangered the entire reconciliation process and threatened the country's institutional fabric. In response to this instability, the government set up a Economic and Social Conciliation Forum, in an effort to bring the government and various social forces together, 'to identify many areas in which we coincide in practice', and to agree social and economic programmes. A major reason why these efforts did not prosper was the lack of any real mechanisms to promote social and political reconciliation. Such mechanisms would have helped to depolarise the situation, by providing more equitable access to and distribution of resources throughout Nicaraguan society. Their absence only generated new forms of political polarisation.

After disarmament: the implementation of the accords

According to figures provided by members of the former *contra*, over 80 per cent of their demobilised soldiers were *campesinos* (peasant farmers), and over 90 per cent of them were illiterate. Within the Sandinista Armed Forces, some 2,000 people were relieved of their duties in the Ministry of the Interior, while the Sandinista Popular Army reduced its troops from 80,000 to about 15,000 in under a year. On both sides, many of these combatants had signed up as adolescents.

The demobilisation process was slow and problematic. Not until 1993, over three years after the elections, did the government announce that it would no longer negotiate with, nor concede amnesty to, any irregular forces still under arms. The International Support and Verification Commission (CIAV) set up by the UN and the Organisation of American States (OAS) to co-ordinate the demobilisation process and the Tela Repatriation Plan, shared responsibility with the office of the UN High Commissioner for Refugees (UNHCR). The latter assumed responsibility for the refugees in neighbouring countries, while the CIAV and OAS took on the demobilisation of members of the National Resistance and their families, provided that these were covered by UNHCR. (The UN organism ONUCA was in charge of recalling and disposing of arms.) CIAV offered a similar assistance package to that of UNHCR, and

repatriated family members of the ex-combatants at a later date. Its mandate was frequently extended for short periods in order to protect the rights and security of the ex-combatants, including verifying and pursuing any claims that these had been violated. Thus CIAV was in practice involved in conflict-mediation and in facilitating dialogue between the conflicting parties.

For the ex-*contra*, the Nicaraguan government established 'development poles', designating specific areas for their resettlement. For the Sandinista Armed Forces, the government planned to offer benefits and allowances according to seniority, as well as training opportunities and certain subsidies. Overall, some 350,000 ex-combatants and their families were eligible for these schemes. According to CIAV, 21,392 members of the ex-National Resistance had been demobilised by July 1991; while by September 1990, 40,000 members of the Sandinista Armed Forces had already been demobilised, and almost 70,000 within the first two years. Ex-*contra* fighters claimed in interviews that their numbers also included their long-term collaborators, civilian supply structures, and others who were keen to get access to the benefits package. The number of registered demobilised *contras* was almost twice the initial estimate, which affected CIAV's financial and logistic capacity. Most of these people remained in the designated 'development poles'. However, conflicts over property, the shortage of funds, and the lack of any specific government commitment to them, meant that these settlements became somewhat unstable. This generated frustration, and led to their continued dependence on CIAV. Among the demobilised Sandinista Armed Forces, the favouritism shown towards higher-ranking officers, and the fact that most regulars lacked the skills necessary to return to civilian life, meant that many of these and their families felt frustrated and had little prospect of employment. According to the Association of Retired Soldiers (AMIR), those who had no kind of support or protection were later to form the bulk of the *recompa* movement, to which we refer again below.

In this situation, the Nicaraguan government marginalised the Peace Plan, rather than focusing on the host of difficulties as a strategic problem. It paid little attention to the commitments already made with the demobilised combatants, or to the efforts of those who were trying to take forward the CIREFCA process, a

UN-sponsored attempt to deal with the problems of refugees and ex-combatants in close collaboration with Nicaraguans themselves. However, by contrast with El Salvador, the Nicaraguan demobilisation process happened very rapidly, and none of the parties involved was truly ready for it. The result was a lack of overall co-ordination which affected both the initial and subsequent phases of the process.

Up to 95 per cent of the Nicaraguan families displaced by the fighting had for years been living in settlements which were supported by the regional governments of their places of origin; a factor which lent them a certain stability. A 1991 survey showed that about 900,000 *campesinos* were still living in 220 such rural settlements. The new government basically ignored the needs of this population and cut subsidised services to them. As part of its new economic policy, the banks reduced the credit available to small producers, which left the co-operatives in these settlements (most of which also had land-titling problems) with no access to credit. The lack of any policies to assist women was particularly striking, given that most displaced and refugee households were female-headed. According to the Association of Nicaraguan Women (AMNLAE), 45 per cent of Nicaraguan households were already headed by women back in 1979, a phenomenon that was greatly accentuated by the war.

The ex-combatants had high expectations of being reintegrated into the rural economy. In addition to the litany of broken promises, the lack of credit and other inputs began to give rise to widespread discontent on both sides. Government statistics show that 1 million acres had been set aside for 15,691 families of the ex-National Resistance; a further 144,000 acres of state-owned land was privatised and allocated to these ex-*contras*, and another 128,000 acres to members of the Sandinista Armed Forces. Yet in practice the allocation of land did not resolve people's survival needs, because legal problems concerning land-titles (which were either non-existent or contested) disqualified them from access to credit and hence denied them the opportunity to earn a living.

When added to the discontent about the government's unkept promises, these practical problems served to encourage the formation of splinter groups. People viewed the high-level agreements as having failed to satisfy the expectations of the *campesinos* who had taken up arms. The high-level negotiations could not — and still cannnot — ensure that reconciliation and demobilisation in the rural areas would become a

nation-wide reality. Despite the general war-weariness and desire for peace, the rapid demobilisation process left little or no time to prepare the rank and file, either politically or psychologically, for what it implied. Given such uncertainty, many ex-combatants and supporters on both sides decided not to turn in their weapons, although there is no means of knowing the exact number who didn't.

The economic crisis was exacerbated by policies that denied most people access to basic services (while allowing some to gain greatly), and the failure to find ways of reintegrating the ex-combatants into society. The resulting tensions culminated in 1994 with unexpectedly high numbers of people taking up arms once again and, in some areas of Nicaragua, embarking on a military offensive. These isolated cases of a return to armed struggle have occasionally taken a bizarre turn, as in the case of the *revueltos* [in Spanish, this play on words means both 'returned' and 'scrambled' — translator's note]. These were rural people from both sides who took up arms again in order to back certain economic demands, but who then demobilised once more. Interestingly, those who were previously enemies joined in attacking the government for failing to address their needs. As late as 1991, some ex-*contras* in the north of the country had resorted to arms in support of their demand for land; and there were cases of Sandinistas responding in like manner. By 1993, there had been 713 armed confrontations, with a total of 1,023 casualties — fairly significant, given that the disarmament process had been completed long before. In response, a National Disarmament Brigade (BED) was formed, though this did not include the various gangs of armed criminals within its scope.

This phenomenon can be explained only by understanding the background and motives of the combatants and their civilian supporters during the war. It is true that the National Resistance was led by Somicista sympathisers. However, during the 1980s, it also attracted support from the peasantry — for instance from farmers who were dissatisfied with the Sandinista agrarian reform policy or who feared that their land might be expropriated. In addition, members of various ethnic minority populations also joined the *contra*. In particular, the Miskito indian population on the Atlantic Coast had been involved in the conflict since they had been forcibly displaced from their homes along the border between Nicaragua and Honduras 'for national security reasons'. The Miskitos had always been marginalised on the political and ideological fringes of national life. Hence, they did not initially identify with the war. For the demobilised troops and their families and supporters, a return to normal civilian life depended on access to the means of production (not merely to land) and work, as well as on maintaining the social and collective achievements following the overthrow of Somoza.

To summarise, while the government did promote some policies to assist ex-combatants, these were largely focused on the military elite and on men, and were not part of any integrated development policy. This 'favouritism' caused considerable feelings of resentment towards the leadership, which was perceived as becoming ever more distant from the needs of ordinary people. The government's economic adjustment policy with cutbacks in social programmes and credit schemes, imposed in order to qualify for World Bank loans, and the failure of many foreign governments to come up with the promised assistance packages, dashed the expectations of the Armed Forces. The ex-*contras* were similarly disappointed by the fact that the development strategies that they had assumed would shape the 'development poles', never materialised. Only now are large-scale programmes being implemented in certain parts of Nicaragua, with support from the multilateral agencies. Currently, neither the government nor the political parties have addressed the question of economic reintegration — or the largely unfulfilled agreements to consider the needs of the ex-combatants.

A decade after the war formally ended, politicians still have to agree on the nature of the transition, perhaps assuming that this has already happened without ever having been addressed. Increasingly, many sectors of Nicaraguan society feel that political leaders have tended to polarise the country rather than contributing to a national climate of peace. This in turn is creating problems for local and regional governments, and leaves a serious credibility (and, therefore, legitimacy) gap at the national level. The state's inability to provide a regulatory framework for its citizens, combined with the lack of resources for investment in the social sector, constitute a real threat to peace. Many people are losing faith in the possibility that their basic problems can be resolved by peaceful means. On the contrary, there is the growing perception that benefits for the poor majority can be gained only through pressure and confrontation.

Civil-society participation in conflict-resolution

Conflict-mediation and resolution initiatives began, as we have already seen, while the war was still raging. As part of its own national policy, the Sandinista government embarked on the Esquipulas process in the hope of finding peaceful solutions, while the internal opposition in Nicaragua began to encourage consensus-building processes which would eventually provide the basis for transition. At the grassroots, people's desire for peace drove many local initiatives to mediate between conflicting parties.

Although the Peace Commissions were officially constituted within the framework of the National Reconciliation Commission (CNR), in practice their dynamic and composition depended on the local context. Gradually, they lost their formal function. Many argue that the Commision's efforts were constrained by the unrelenting opposition of the Catholic hierarchy towards the Sandinistas, which tainted its impartiality. Nevertheless, local political leaders and members of the church joined the Peace Commissions in an effort to reproduce the CNR initiative. Sometimes these local commissions succeeded in encouraging people to come forward and seek amnesty. Such occasions were the only experience of active civil-society participation in the entire reconciliation process.

In the final years of the Sandinista government, the UN-sponsored CIREFCA process attempted to focus attention on the population directly affected by the conflicts, and to channel resources to them. CIREFCA also served to bring together the efforts of national and international NGOs. Nicaraguan NGOs seized the opportunity to play an active part in resettling and reintegrating refugees and enabled people to talk with the international actors who were supporting them. This creative and energetic engagement by national NGOs in high-level political dialogue is considered a unique achievement. However, although these efforts still continue, the absence of any clear government policy towards the displaced, the lack of resources, and the problems faced by NGOs in the transition period, have meant that the response has fallen far short of meeting the need.

After 1990, only a few organisations in Nicaragua have deliberately worked in conflict-resolution and mediation. However, ex-combatants themselves have set up spontaneous projects, sometimes in connection with Church-based initiatives. In addition — while these have not necessarily been described as conflict-resolution programmes — NGOs such as CEPAD (a church-based agency), the Augusto Cesar Sandino Foundation (FACS), and others have acted as facilitators in conflicts which arose in their areas of work. However, these activities have generally responded to a specific problem rather than being as part of a planned strategy. Other programmes have aimed to address the needs of certain groups (women and young people in particular) within an overall framework of consensus-building.

The local Peace Commissions were — and still are in some areas — particularly important, because they offer innovative ways for citizens to participate in conflict-resolution. Their efforts at the grassroots level have proven more effective than more formal mechanisms, and the commisions have played a key role in facilitating dialogue. For example, in Waslala and Esteli, local people appealed to both sides in the conflict to negotiate, putting themselves forward as mediators.

Given the lack of response to their demands, some ex-combatants formed mixed commissions to manage particular projects and negotiate on their behalf, both with the international aid agencies and with the government. Again, these have worked mainly at the local level. The national organisations of ex-combatants have have largely maintained their war-time identity or political affiliation, but even so, they have collaborated in putting forward certain demands. Here, the experience of the Peasant Alliance is interesting, since it represents a cautious alliance between the Union of Farmers and Cattle-ranchers (UNAG), which had always been seen as a Sandinista stronghold, and the Association of Resistance Commandos (ACOR). While modest, this alliance represents a real advance in building a basis of common interest between former adversaries.

The International Studies Centre (CEI) is one of the few Nicaraguan organisations which has worked directly with demobilised fighters and soldiers, offering leadership training in particular. Founded in 1991, the CEI acts as a facilitation centre, where ex-combatants from both sides can meet, and receive training and follow-up in conflict-resolution. While the CEI does not believe in the concept of neutrality (its directors were once senior members of the Sandinista government), it sets its work within the ethical framework of *recovering one's identity* as a key factor in returning to civilian life. It has succeeded in bringing together former military leaders, and mainly works at the leadership level via the ex-combatants' own organisations.

The Nueva Guinea co-operative

Clearly, the reconciliation efforts at the national level, which depended more on formal structures, were quite different from those that have been so significant at the grassroots level. The experiences of FACS and CEPAD in the Nueva Guinea region of the Atlantic Coast have been quite unique, largely because both institutions had worked there prior to efforts to re-integrate the ex-combatants. For instance, a co-operative was made up of local families who had returned from refugee camps in Honduras and Costa Rica. They were later joined by ex-combatants from both sides, as well as by people who had fled the violence in the north of the country. In 1990, the year in which the *contras* in the area were demobilised, various national and international NGOs were supporting this work. At present, there are some 56 families in the co-operative. They coexist peacefully and farm the land together — perhaps the only such experience in the country. In addition, about 420 war-maimed ex-combatants from both sides work together in the same area, alongside other families who were displaced by the fighting.

Nueva Guinea was the first experience of a reconciliation process which actually worked in practice, and where the armed conflicts came to a complete halt as a result. Admittedly, some ex-*contras* tried to re-arm in 1992 (probably at the instigation of one of the political parties), and the community suffered some fatalities, as well as conflicts over land, and cases of dispossession of some co-operative members. However, the people and the organisations living alongside the fighting parties worked energetically to convince everyone of the need for peace, and succeeded in ensuring that the conflicts went no futher.

The relative success of this co-operative has obviously given a great boost to an area that in other respects suffers the same poverty as the rest of the country. The reasons for its success are quite complex, and must be set in the context of the community's own organisational history. First, the ex-combatants who settled in Nueva Guinea had not fought there during the war. This perhaps defused the resentment that local people might otherwise have felt towards them, as well as tensions among themselves. Moreover, when the co-operative was established, ex-combatants from both sides were deliberately included in its leadership. People say that in the first meeting, the ex-fighters were so distrustful that they remained armed, even though they had formally demobilised. Another important factor was the effort of the various NGOs and grassroots organ-isations in the area (UNAG, CEPAD, FACS, the

Mothers of Heroes and Martyrs, AMNLAE, the chuch, and the communal movement) to work in a co-ordinated fashion, despite the fact that the existence of such diverse organisations in one place often creates problems for the beneficiaries. Unfortunately, the international aid agencies working there did not make similar efforts to work together. As a result, it was difficult for them effectively to set priorities and to target their assistance.

The government did not initially promote any reconciliation projects such as the one in Nueva Guinea. But with NGO assistance, an agricultural and technical aid programme was started. The successful detente probably owed much to the fact that there was a good harvest.

But at least it showed that collective effort could yield results, and also reduced the additional pressure on resources. It was equally important to reach a consensus on what people felt were their most pressing needs, and to engage in peace-building activities which involved the aid agencies, the local people, community leaders from the FSLN and the National Resistance, and from the evangelical church. Another factor which defused conflicts and also facilitated co-ordination was that no one tried to force changes in people's own organisational structures, even including the military structures. This created a climate of respect, based on acknowledging the characteristics and identity of each individual.

Table 1: Chronology of the peace process in Nicaragua

Year	Event	Consequences	Civil-society participation
1983	Governments of Colombia, Mexico, Panama, Venezuela form Contadora Group to discuss peace plans		
1984	Talks on Atlantic Coast autonomy		
	Elections	Sandinista government wins 67% of the vote	
1985	US president Reagan declares trade embargo		
1987	Esquipulas meetings with UN and OAS involvement to reach peace accord		
1988	Government participates in Esquipulas II accord	Regional and local Peace Commissions set up	National Reconciliation Commission established by the Catholic church; civil-society participation in Peace Commissions
	Internal opposition calls for national dialogue	National Opposition Union (UNO), a 14-party coalition, formed	
1989	Tela Summit and signing of 'Joint Plan for the Demobilisation, Voluntary Repatriation or Relocation in Nicaragua or in Third Countries of Members of the National Resistance and their Families'	Material and security conditions agreed for demobilised soldiers and fighters, with international collaboration; amnesty for ex-combatants implicit; no advances in demobilisation	
	Sapoá Accord		
	Informal channnels of communication set up between *contra* and Sandinista military leaders, in advance of Institutional Policy Accords		Civil-society reconciliation initiatives

25

Table 1: Chronology of the peace process in Nicaragua *continued*

Year	Event	Consequences	Civil-society participation
1990	Transition Accord signed	No clear social or economic commitments	
	Elections	UNO win elections	
		Demobilisation of RN commences	
	Government announces that it will no longer grant amnesty to irregular fighters still under arms		
	UNHCR responsible for refugees in neighbouring countries; CIAV responsible for demoblisation of RN and their families	UNHCR and CIAV mandates extended to protect rights and security of ex-combatants	
	ONUCA charged with recalling and disposing of arms	Violations of accords verified	
	CIAV responsible for subsequent repatriation of disarmed contras	CIAV involved in conflict-mediation and facilitation of dialogue	
	'Development poles' established for ex-RN		
	Sandinista Armed Forces base benefits package on seniority	CIAV lacks logistical and financial resources to meet demands	
	Association of Retired Soldiers (AMIR) forms *recompa* movement	Impossible to ascertain extent of involvement of AMIR in *recompa* movement	
	Frustration with broken commitments leads to local outbreaks of fighting	Co-government established	
	Protocol for the transfer of presidential power	Government sets up forum for Economic and Social Concertation, but no mechanisms established for Social Reconciliation	
1991 – 92	Mass strikes		
	Isolated cases of return to arms		
	Revueltos take to arms		
1993	713 military actions	1,023 casualties	
	National Disarmament Brigade formed		
	Government designs policies to boost leadership, but without a vision of integrated development		
	Lack of agreement on nature of transition required at institutional level		
1994	Amnesty granted to all rebels in order to encourage disarmament		

EL SALVADOR

Background

Many Salvadorans believe that the armed conflict which came to a head in the 1980s originated in the insurrection of 1932. This had culminated in the slaughter of hundreds of *campesinos* and shaped the policies of successive military governments thereafter, repressing all political dissent. In 1980 the Christian Democrat Party (PCD), which represented private business, and high-ranking military officers formed a new government, at a time when popular opposition to the government was gaining strength both in the form of a mass movement and in the guerrilla forces that had emerged in the 1970s. A strong alliance between them was forged in response to the the US and Salvadoran governments' handling of the conflict and to the kind of society they envisaged.

Two factors were to characterise the nature of the war and its negotiated solution. First, the US was an active protagonist in the counter-insurgency effort, providing significant economic and political support for the Salvadoran government, and being directly involved in defining military strategy. From the late 1970s, in the face of growing opposition, the PCD began talks with the military and with the US government, with a view to getting their support for a new civilian-military Junta from which other groups, including civil-society organisations, would be excluded.

'Thus, the US attempted to instal a flexible government in El Salvador, that would serve its own geo-political and geo-strategic interests in Central America. This buried the possibility of a coup d'état by the hard-liners in the military, beyond the Pentagon's control. Equally, the military could stop the Salvadoran guerrillas from becoming the new Sandinistas, and El Salvador the next Nicaragua in Central America.' (Oscar Martinez Penate, *El Salvador: Del Conflicto Armado a la Negociación 1979–1989*)

The US policy was geared to goal of eradicating any opposition, armed or peaceful. According to the Reagan Administration's own statistics, 800 politically motivated murders were commited each month during 1980; between 1980 and 1981 alone, about 8,200 trade unionists were killed.

Successive military governments, as well as the elected governments of Duarte and Cristiani, used political repression as a means to discourage the opposition — which greatly affected the population at large. Political repression — part of the so-called 'low-intensity' conflict — was sometimes combined with social and economic reforms (such as the Agrarian Reform), which were intended to neutralise the armed opposition and its sympathisers.

On 10 January 1980, the guerrilla organisations went public with their first joint manifesto, announcing a political alliance with the Revolutionary Co-ordination of the Masses (CRM) and calling for revolutionary struggle. Later, the CRM was joined by the unions, representatives of small and medium-sized businesses, various political parties, the University of El Salvador, and the Association of Transport Workers, among others. Together, they formed the Democratic Revolutionary Front (FDR), acknowledging the guerrilla organisations' Unified Direction (DU) group as 'the vanguard', and accepting its direction of the Salvadoran revolution. This broad-based alliance between the FMLN and the FDR enjoyed immense popular support in El Salvador, and also opened up the possibility of significant diplomatic backing on the international stage. In January 1981, the Political Commission of the FDR-FMLN was formed, a body which was to play a key role in peace negotiations in El Salvador.

In the same month, the FMLN launched a military offensive which was intended to lead to a popular insurrection. Although it did not succeed in this aim, the offensive nevertheless marked a new phase in the war. By then, the government's repression was directed not only against the armed opposition but against the entire popular movement, especially with the emergence of para-military groups known as 'death squads'. According to Americas Watch, 38,000 of the 50,000 people killed during the war were non-combatants. Many of them were tortured by the security forces. Some 70,000 people were killed between 1980 and 1989, while more than 1 million Salvadorans left the country, and hundreds more became displaced.

The peace negotiation process

The first mediation efforts

From the early 1980s, the negotiated solution to the liberation war in Zimbabwe was cited as a model for ending the conflict in El Salvador. However, negotiation would have depended on the willingness of the Junta, the FMLN-FDR, the US government, and the UN to participate actively, based on an agreement on the central issues and problems to be addressed. Had this happened, the process would have been guaranteed by international observers, and by the threat of sanctions if the commitments were flouted. However, at the time the FMLN-FDR were less interested in elections than in negotiating the conditions for their full participation in the Junta, while the PDC and the Armed Forces insisted that they disarm as a pre-condition for negotiation. The UN was 'convinced ... that at the present time the conditions for holding genuinely democratic elections did not exist in El Salvador' (UN Resolution for the First Quarter of 1981). So, repeated attempts at international mediation stalled, and were even viewed by the Salvadoran government, the military, and other sectors as interference in the country's internal affairs.

In early 1981, the Latin America and Caribbean Committee of the Socialist International met in Panama, at the invitation of General Omar Torrijos. The Committee reiterated its willingness to mediate between the FMLN-FDR and the PDC-military Junta. The former responded positively, but the Junta and the US Administration rejected the proposal, arguing that the pre-condition for dialogue was that the FMLN disarm. In April the Vice-President of the Socialist International, Edward Broadbent, led a peace mission to seek a negotiated solution. In his final report, he concluded that peace would be possible only if the US government were prepared to change its policy — an idea rejected by the Reagan Administration. The government of the German Federal Republic offered to mediate, but was also turned down by the USA. In response to the deadlock, the Christian Democrat group within the European Union Parliament invited members of the Socialist International to analyse the possiblities for a negotiated peace settlement in El Salvador. The then president of the Junta, Duarte, reiterated his rejection of any form of international mediation, insisting that the country's internal problems had to be resolved by the Salvadorans themselves 'without external intervention'. The Canadian government also offered its mediation services, with the same results.

By then, various Latin American governments were also voicing concern about the Salvadoran conflict. Several communiqués and mediation proposals expressed their fear that the war might assume international proportions. In February 1981, the president of Costa Rica, Rodrigo Carazo, proposed that the Organisation of American States (OAS) offer to facilitate dialogue between the FMLN-FDR and the Junta; to which the Salvadoran government responded that it did not consider that the OAS was legally equipped for this role. In April, the governments of Mexico and Venezuela again offered to mediate; an offer that was once again turned down by the Salvadoran Junta, along with two further offers from the Costa Rican president made before the UN General Assembly, and another offer from the government of Ecuador.

The Catholic church played an active part throughout the entire process. In September 1980, months after the assassination of Archbishop Romero, it, too, offered to mediate through the Episcopal Conference. However, the military insisted that the FMLN-FDR must lay down arms before dialogue could commence, and the latter rejected the proposal, arguing that Catholic hierarchy was aligned with the Junta. Other international efforts to achieve peace included that of the US National Council of Churches, which recommended a negotiated solution after a delegation had visited El Salvador.

In October 1981, Mexico and Venezuela issued a joint declaration which was supported by 43 parties within the Socialist International. Their recognition of the FMLN-FDR as a representative political force represented an immense support, and marked the political distance between the US government's position and international opinion. The Franco-Mexican Declaration advocated a negotiated solution, while the Reagan Administration favoured an electoral one. Duarte viewed this Declaration as an external interference in internal affairs. The US government made no direct response, but supported the Caracas Declaration of various military and right-wing Latin American governments, which expressed their support for the Salvadoran Junta.

The FMLN-FDR repeatedly affirmed their wish to open a dialogue with the Junta, provided that this was mediated internationally, and that there were no preconditions concerning the laying down of arms. At the October 1981 meeting of the UN General Assembly the FMLN-FDR proposed an agenda for opening peace negotiations, through Nicaragua's Comandante Daniel Ortega. This too was rejected by the Salvadoran Junta.

In the USA, certain sectors which had been influenced by the Carter Administration's earlier policies, proposed that the FMLN-FDR be recognised, and that the US government abandon confrontation in favour of negotiation, and reduce its direct involvement in the war. The FMLN-FDR had announced their wish to negotiate with the US government as early as December 1980, even before the outbreak of the war. The Carter Administration had put forward certain negotiating points, but these were rejected by the left — both because they expected the 1981 offensive to unleash a popular insurrection, and because they were convinced that the Reagan Administration would not honour any undertakings. Following the military offensive, the FMLN-FDR again called for negotiations, but this time Washington refused. The Episcopal Conference reiterated its call for dialogue, to which the FMLN-FDR responded favourably; but the proposal received no official response from the government or the military.

On 28 March 1982, elections were held for the Constituent Assembly that was to draft the new Constitution. Only right-wing and centre parties participated in these elections, which were held during a state of siege. The PDC won a relative majority. The leader of the extreme right-wing ARENA party, Major Roberto D'Aubuisson, brought together like-minded parties in an opposition alliance.

The Socialist International recognised that the 1982 elections had not resolved the conflict. However, they showed that the US government would not allow a right-wing government which excluded the PDC, since its policy towards El Salvador would lose credibility if political forces associated with the death squads were to become too powerful. In a meeting with Salvadoran political leaders, the US government offered to suspend economic and military aid if Major D'Aubuisson were made provisional president. In response, the Armed Forces chose Alvaro Magaña, a member of the right-wing PCN. The political right wing in El Salvador accepted this, on condition that the US government accept D'Aubuisson as President of the Constituent Assembly.

On 2 May 1982, Magaña became President; and various agreements were ratified, including the Apaneca Pact, in which the political parties within the Junta agreed to refrain from attacking each other, and to form a common front against the FMLN-FDR — who were again called on to lay down arms. This Pact proposed setting up a Peace Commission, the main aim of which would be to propose solutions for social stability. It also proposed establishing a Human Rights Commission, whose members would include the head of the National Police — an institution accused of being one of the worst violators of human rights. This Commission passed an Amnesty Law in May 1983, which meant that no criminal proceedings could be taken against those responsible for the assassination of Archbishop Romero, or for killing four American nuns, among many others. The Pact further included the creation of a Political Commission under the co-ordination of Magaña, the Armed Forces, and the united right-wing parties. This Commission was to govern El Salvador until the next presidential elections. By then, the war had already claimed over 40,000 lives.

That same month, the FMLN-FDR proposed holding direct negotiations in the USA to seek a solution to the armed conflict. While there was some American interest, the initiative was aborted because of what the FMLN-FDR referred to as disagreements over 'procedures' (10 July 1983 FMLN-FDR communiqué). Other initiatives followed, such as that of Colombian President Betancur, which resulted in an initial meeting between delegates from the US government and the FMLN-FDR, in which they agreed to meet once more. This took place in August 1983, but failed because neither side was prepared to compromise.

On 5 June 1983, the FMLN-FDR published a five-point proposal in which it reiterated its willingness to seek a negotiated solution, but questioned the legitimacy and representative nature of the Peace Commission. Both the US and the Salvadoran governments ignored this, since both wanted to pursue indirect dialogue through the Peace Commission. The FMLN-FDR were thus forced to communicate with the Commission, and a first meeting was held in Bogota in August 1983, with a follow-up meeting scheduled in Panama.

However, the Peace Commission did not attend the second meeting, but unilaterally fixed the next meeting for September 1983, again in Bogota. Here, the FMLN-FDR repeated their five-point proposal for open dialogue with various sectors of society, and the formation of a transition government (in which it would participate) to create the conditions for free and democratic elections. The Commission asked the FMLN-FDR to participate in the 1984 elections, as long as it acknowledged the government in power. The FMLN-FDR rejected this proposal and ended the dialogue.

In January 1984, the FMLN-FDR set out a detailed proposal for general elections and the formation of a provisional government made up of a Junta, a ministerial cabinet, and a supreme court of justice. The proposal included the derogation of the 1983 Constitution; recognition of the legitimacy of popular power in the areas under FMLN military control; a purge of the Armed Forces with an investigation of accusations of human-rights violations; the exclusion of representatives of the oligarchy from the government; and the dissolution of the ARENA party. Once again, there was no official response, while the US government and the united right-wing front insisted that the FMLN-FDR participate in the elections to be held on 25 March 1984.

The PDC fielded Napoleon Duarte as their presidential candidate, in a campaign which stressed that to vote for him was to vote for dialogue. The ARENA candidate was Roberto D'Aubuisson. The FMLN-FDR declined to participate. Duarte and the PDC were standing for a project that had been conceived by and enjoyed the support of the US government (it is claimed that the USA invested some US$10 million in Duarte's campaign), while D'Aubuisson and ARENA represented the interests of the Salvadoran oligarchy. Both tried to discredit the FMLN-FDR as a political force. However, the widespread national and international contempt felt for D'Aubuisson, because of his involvement with the 'death squads', entailed a high political cost for the US government and threatened to discredit its Central American policy.

Duarte was returned as president for the 1984–89 period, in elections that were held in 173 of the country's 262 municipalities, excluding those under FMLN military control. ARENA condemned the USA's involvement in supporting the PDC, and D'Aubuisson claimed that the elections were not legitimate since they had been won by the CIA. His position caused further clashes with the US Administration, and marked the beginning of the latter's gradual shift towards a negotiated solution.

Electoral processes and proposals for dialogue

Once elected, Duarte embarked on a major international tour during which he stressed his willingness to enter into peace negotiations, but not to share power with the FMLN-FDR. He also insisted that external mediation was unnecessary, saying that 'Contadora is an organism made up of four countries which believe they have the right to intervene in the area' (El Día, 4 July 1984). He won major economic and diplomatic support from the UK and the German Federal Republic; and, in a joint communiqué, Reagan and Duarte stated their support for democracies and electoral processes in the region.

Before Duarte took up office, the FMLN had underlined its wish to negotiate, calling for him to stop American involvement in the war, to halt bombings of civilians, and to bring an end to political detention, murders, and disappearances (May 1984 FMLN proposal). However, the FDR saw Duarte as a potential interlocutor, and stated its willingness to begin an open-ended dialogue. Duarte reiterated that he would not contemplate any power-sharing arrangement, and called for the FMLN to disarm.

Over the next four years, four formal dialogues took place between the FMLN-FDR, the PDC, and the Salvadoran Armed Forces, only two of which achieved any concrete results. Essentially, the FMLN-FDR sought access to political power through negotiation, while their interlocutors (and the US government) saw dialogue as complementing their counter-insurgency strategy.

The first of these meetings took place at La Palma in FMLN-held territory in the north of the country in October 1984, following an invitation to the FMLN (not the FDR) by President Duarte issued the previous week before during a speech at the UN General Assembly. The Reagan Administration felt that this showed Duarte as favouring a negotiated solution, and would therefore reduce the growing opposition to its policy on El Salvador and allay the American public's fear of 'another Vietnam'. Archbishop Rivera y Damas would moderate, and other bishops were to act as witnesses.

The meeting took place in the church, behind closed doors. Both sides reiterated their existing positions, and the FMLN was again asked to hand over their arms in return for a general amnesty and the possibility of becoming a political party. However, Duarte's suggestion of establishing a mixed commission to examine the various peace proposals, to be moderated by the Episcopal Conference, was accepted.

This dialogue appeared to guarantee the future of the FMLN-FDR and showed the government's willingness to negotiate. However, only three days later, the Armed Forces launched the largest ever military offensive against the FMLN. The 'death squads', which had always been opposed to dialogue, condemned the meeting as a farce. But the La Palma dialogue did nevertheless give ordinary people the opportunity to express their support for dialogue and peace, without fearing that repression would automatically follow, and to legitimise their opinions both within El Salvador and on an international stage.

Even before La Palma, both sides had agreed to a second meeting, during a televised debate in the USA. This took place in Ayagualo in November 1984, with representatives of the Salvadoran Episcopal Conference, headed by Mons. Rivera y Damas, once again acting as witnesses and intermediaries. This time the FMLN-FDR proposed a three-step process for resolving the armed conflict: the first referred to international humanitarian law; the second to the suspension of hostilities in order to allow for peace and for disarmament; and the third to creating the institutional framework for democracy, as the outcome of dialogue and negotiation. The government delegation rejected this, arguing that this would violate the Constitution. Instead, directing its proposal exclusively at the FMLN, it called for them to lay down their arms, return to democratic society in El Salvador, participate in the next round of legislative and municipal elections, and respect the political Constitution. The FMLN-FDR rejected this, arguing that it amounted to surrender, and that it did not address the problem of human-rights violations. Nevertheless, it was agreed to establish the Mixed Commission, to permit the evacuation of FMLN casualties, and to continue the dialogue. But Duarte never fulfilled these commitments, arguing that Legislative Assembly did not support them. The FMLN, however, handed over to the Church 42 soldiers it had been holding prisoner since 1984.

The FMLN-FDR's call for a third meeting in Perquín came to nothing, although Duarte did express his willingness to hold private and public meetings outside El Salvador. By then, the Episcopal Conference had also released its Pastoral Letter calling for peace and reconciliation in which it expressed public support for the PDC, the Armed Forces, and the USA, accusing the FMLN and left-wing opposition groups of being responsible for lack of progress in the dialogue. After this, the Church could no longer mediate because it was viewed as partisan. Nonetheless, the FMLN repeated its Ayagualo dialogue proposal, albeit with no outcome.

In September 1985, the situation reached a critical point when the FMLN kidnapped one of Duarte's daughters, Guadalupe Duarte (although they initially denied responsibility). Eventually, the FMLN agreed to release her as well as 23 mayors and municipal functionaries kidnapped earlier. The PDC agreed to free 22 political prisoners, including the FMLN Comandante Nidia Díaz. But the kidnapping of Duarte's daughter put a severe strain on relations, and effectively paralysed the negotiation process for the next two years.

In March 1986, the PDC government said that it would hold a dialogue with the FDR-FMLN if the Sandinista government in Nicaragua simultaneously met with the irregular forces or *contra*; this coincided with the Reagan Administration's request to Congress to approve US$100 million for the *contra*. The FDR-FMLN held various private meetings with the PDC, mediated by President Alan Garcia of Peru, to plan a meeting between the PDC leadership and the parties belonging to the FDR. The representatives of two of these, the MNR and the MPSC, discussed the possibility of a meeting with the PDC and the Armed Forces. The government's responded by calling on these to abandon the FMLN and participate in the elections slated for late 1988.

Throughout 1986, the FDR-FMLN made various fruitless proposals, as did Duarte, all of which were mediated by Mons. Rivera y Damas. By August, a third meeting appeared possible, because both sides had shown increased flexibility on certain issues: the FMLN in relation to the punishment of military officers, and the government in relation to a meeting on Salvadoran territory. Both parties agreed to proceed with preparatory meetings, the first of which took place in Mexico and ratified the agreements reached in La Palma and Ayagualo. The third meeting was to be held in Sesori to discuss the FDR-FMLN's latest proposals. However, the town was full of government forces, and the FDR-FMLN refused to participate under such conditions. The government delegation, accompanied by guests from the US Embassy, claimed that this showed the FMLN's lack of political will to reach a negotiated settlement.

31

In May 1987, the FDR-FMLN presented an 18-point proposal which was ignored by the Salvadoran government. In October 1987, four days after the signing of the Esquipulas II Accords, the FDR-FMLN again proposed a dialogue. This time, Duarte responded favourably and a meeting was held that same month, mediated by Mons. Rivera y Damas and witnessed by the Papal Nuncio. The items on the agenda included: the Esquipulas II accords, and a political solution to the conflict; the position on non-violence; 'forgiving and forgetting' as part of the political solution; specific agreements concerning a political solution; and the establishment of a process of dialogue and joint communications. The new element was that both sides were by this time making these proposals in the context of Esquipulas II. In accordance with the Esquipulas framework, two commissions were established, each made up of four representatives from both sides, to prepare cease-fire agreements and other points relating to the Accords.

The two commissions met in August 1987 in Venezuela, but without reaching significant agreements. Days later, the president of the Salvadoran Human Rights Commission, Herbert Anaya, was assassinated. In response, the FDR-FMLN unilaterally called off any dialogue with the government. Six months later, the FDR-FMLN sought to re-open dialogue via the two commissions, but the government refused. The situation became more complicated for the FMLN when the FDR decided to become a political party, just as Duarte was rejecting any dialogue. It thus embarked on a diplomatic offensive, particularly in Europe, and launched a major offensive on the military front.

By 1988, peace was already one of the main political campaign themes. The extreme right-wing party ARENA, which had always opposed dialogue or negotiation with the FDR-FMLN, suddenly declared itself in favour of a negotiated solution. A new element in the electoral campaign was the Democratic Convergence, a coalition of the former FDR and the Social Democrats.

The FMLN proposed to meet the government, as long as this was postponed from March to September 1989. When an FMLN proposal that would allow for communication with all political parties (except ARENA) did not prosper, the FMLN urged Salvadorans to reject the elections. With an abstention rate of about 65 per cent, Alfredo Cristiani of the ARENA party was brought to power. For the second time, a civilian president was returned against a backdrop of acute armed conflict and violent political repression.

The final offensive and the start of negotiation

Alfredo Cristiani took office on 1 June 1989. During the first few months he showed some willingness to enter into dialogue with the FMLN, but failed to take any concrete steps. The FMLN likewise showed some willingness to take up dialogue, although it had previously argued that the ARENA government was not legitimate, and that it would not negotiate with the Salvadoran oligarchy.

In May 1989, the FMLN proposed resuming the dialogue, but received no official response. However, it unilaterally suspended its acts of economic sabotage, and called on the government to play its part in creating a climate that would favour dialogue and negotiation. Eventually, it was agreed that both sides would meet in Mexico in September 1989. Under pressure from the most conservative parts of ARENA, the Catholic Church did not mediate as it had done under Duarte, but acted only as witness.

In Mexico, the FMLN again wanted to negotiate the question of UN and OAS verification, punishment for those guilty of human-rights violations, and constitutional reforms. The ARENA delegation wanted to discuss the procedures for pushing ahead with dialogue and negotiation. Eventually it was agreed that there would be a negotiated cease-fire, and that ordinary meetings would be held one month later in order to allow for consultation and the formulation of concrete proposals. It was also agreed to invite two members of the Salvadoran Episcopal Conference as witnesses, as well as representatives of international organisations; and to establish ways of communicating with and consulting the political parties and social forces. It was further agreed that there would be no unilateral suspension of the dialogue process; and that the next meeting would concentrate on the cease-fire, with the OAS and UN as witnesses.

On 11 October 1989, the FMLN proposed that peace negotiations should take place in El Salvador. The government and military delegation responded five days later, just as the three-day meeting in San Jose was about to begin. The response was largely positive, except for points relating to the investigation and punishment of those responsible for the assassination of Archbishop Romero, the 'death squads', and the purging of the Armed Forces. A programme for a cease-fire and for international verification of compliance with the Accords were both agreed.

The next meeting was scheduled to take place in Caracas in November 1989, to be attended by respresentatives of the UN and the OAS. Thus, the ARENA government was on the one hand showing greater flexibility towards the possibility of dialogue, while on the other intensifying its attacks on the opposition — these were directed not only against the Democratic Convergence and popular organisations, but also at grassroots organisations and civilian settlements in the conflict zones.

On 11 November 1989, the FMLN launched another military offensive which sought to provoke a popular insurrection in order to give rise to a transition government in which it would also participate. This offensive, which was largely concentrated in San Salvador, did not gain as much popular support as expected. In addition, the social and political cost was very high: more than 1,000 civilians died and, according to official figures, some 30,000 homes were damaged or destroyed. However, the offensive showed the Salvadoran and international public that the FMLN was not a militarily spent force, as the US government and the Salvadoran Armed Forces had believed. It also demonstrated that the ARENA government and the Armed Forces were guilty of systematic human-rights violations against the civilian population. (Some were also committed by the FMLN, but on a far lesser scale.) The offensive also served to put El Salvador back on the international agenda, which was then dominated by events in the Middle East.

The government and Armed Forces then embarked on a campaign of ferocious persecution of the leaders of the political parties that had been in the FDR. As a result, many of these either went into exile or underground. The authorities also attacked leaders and rank-and-file members of the popular organisations — for example, bombing and ransacking their offices, killing ten people in one such raid — as well as those of NGOs. They pursued church leaders and congregations, as well as international aid workers and representatives, whom they accused of supporting the FMLN. However, the greatest national and international outrage was caused by the assassination, in cold blood, of six Jesuits, all highly respected intellectuals, along with two of their assistants. The decision to murder them was taken by a group of soldiers, and it later emerged US advisers were complicit in the plan. While the Salvadoran government committed itself to investigating the crime, those responsible were never officially identified.

The international revulsion generated by this assassination and by the fierce repression, as well as the results of the offensive itself, convinced the US government, ARENA, and the Armed Forces that it was useless to continue the war. These factors were also to determine the FMLN's negotiation strategy. The determination of the US solidarity movement, which had undertaken advocay work in the US Congress for many years, also began to bear fruit; and those who had most strongly supported the idea of a military solution came under increasing pressure. The impact this had on many US politicians, particularly the Democrats, meant that the strategy followed by Reagan and later Bush gradually began to include the idea of dialogue, and to draw back from seeing a military solution as the only option.

Negotiation

During the September and December 1989 negotiating rounds, the Bush Administration approached the Group of Friends of the UN Secretary-General. This helped to overcome the resistance to a negotiated solution that still existed within the upper echelons of the military and the ARENA party.

In a meeting of the Central American presidents that took place after the FMLN offensive, Cristiani accepted the good offices role of a representative of the UN Secretary-General in intervening to open up negotiations. On 4 April 1990, the Framework Agreement was signed at the UN headquarters in New York. The Salvadoran government asked the FMLN to put forward substantive proposals, to which it would then respond. This helped to deflect the likelihood of serious conflicts within ARENA, in view of the potential resistance even to the process of agreeing the topics for negotiation. It also allowed the FMLN to define the main content of the negotiations, and to shape the resulting accords. For the FMLN, the main objective was '… to open the path towards democracy', while it remained their priority to abolish the military dictatorship and reform the Armed Forces (*The long process leading to war and negotiation in El Salvador*, Schafik Jorge Handal, 1996).

In Geneva, Switzerland, the two parties agreed an agenda with four central negotiating objectives: a political solution to the armed conflict; democracy in El Salvador; assurances guaranteeing respect for human rights; and the re-uniting of Salvadoran society. In three further meetings between July 1990 and September 1991, agreements were reached which eventually led to the signing of the Peace Accords in Mexico in January 1992. (The contents of the Accord are summarised in Appendix 1.)

Today, most observers agree that these Accords opened up a space for political participation by the opposition forces within El Salvador, and therefore represented a huge step forward in terms of democratisation. But while the Land Transfer Programme to ex-

combatants and *de facto* land-holders in the former conflict zones is still in progress, the peace process has been a constant struggle for local people and grassroots organisations. Similarly, any degree of government compliance with the Peace Accords has been the result of constant pressure. The real vacuum, however, is in the social and economic spheres. As a result of the way in which the Peace Accords were implemented, in practice they have achieved relatively little for most Salvadorans.

Table 2: Chronology of peace negotiations in El Salvador

Year	Event	Results	Civil-society participation
1984	FMLN-FDR propose dialogue with Duarte via Mons. Rivera y Damas	No response; Duarte refuses to negotiate until FMLN lays down arms	
	FMLN-FDR ask US Senator Jesse Jackson for a reply		
	Duarte calls the FMLN-FDR to a meeting in La Palma; USA approves of proposed meeting, which is moderated by Mons. Rivera y Damas with other religious authorities as witnesses	FMLN agrees and proposes President Betancur of Colombia to intervene; Duarte accepts	La Palma meeting opens space for Salvadorans to express themselves openly on peace proposals
	Duarte proposes mixed commission to study the peace proposals, to be moderated by Mons. Rivera y Damas	FMLN-FDR accept Mixed Commission	
	Ayagualo meeting	Mixed commission formed; FMLN casualties evacuated; dialogue resumes	
	FMLN-FDR propose third meeting in Perquín	Perquín meeting does not take place	
1985	Duarte's daughter kidnapped and then released with 23 local mayors. PDC promises to release 22 political prisoners	Peace process paralysed for two years	
1986	Lima: Meetings in which FDR is asked to leave the FMLN and participate in elections		
	PDC shows intention to meet with FMLN-FDR		
	Preparatory meetings held		
	Mexico: La Palma and Ayagualo Accords ratified		
1987	FDR-FMLN make 18-point proposal	No response	
	Esquipulas II signed	Proposals made in Esquipulas II context to support peace process and setting up of National Reconciliation Commissions, with proposed cease-fire agreement	

Table 2: Chronology of peace negotiations in El Salvador *continued*

Year	Event	Results	Civil-society participation
1987	FDR-FMLN proposes dialogue: Duarte accepts		
	Two commissions meet in Venezuela: days later, FDR-FMLN break off dialogue following the assassination of Herbert Anaya, president of non-government human rights commission	No major agreements	
1988	FDR-FMLN request government to resume dialogue	Government rejects proposal	
	Political parties in FDR join in elections in coalition with PSD (social democrats)	Democratic Convergence party formed	
	FMLN proposes meetings, without success	FMLN asks the population to reject the elections	
1989	FMLN proposes resumption of dialogue	No response	
	FMLN suspends economic sabotage and calls on government to create climate of dialogue and negotiation	Agreement to meet in Mexico in September	
	Meeting in Mexico	Both delegations accept UN and OAS verification; Episcopal Conference called as witness; consultation process set up with political parties; agreement reached to meet in San José	
	FMLN propose peace negotiations to resume in El Salvador	Response to FMLN proposal agreed	
	San José meeting	Cease-fire agreed, with international verification of observance of accords; meeting in Venezuela with UN and OAS officials invited	Persecution of political opposition, members of popular organisations, churches, unions etc. intensifies, as does that of civilians in conflict zones
	FMLN launches military offensive	Cost of military offensive: 1000 dead, 30 000 homes lost or damaged	
		Bloodshed demonstrates uselessness of armed conflict and shapes the future negotiation process	Six Jesuit priests and their assistants killed in cold blood
1989 /90	President Cristiani accepts UN mediation	Framework Accord signed at UN headquarters to cover end of armed conflict, democratisation process, respect for human rights, reunification of Salvadoran society	Permanent Committee for National Dialogue (CPDN), made up of broad range of social groupings, makes statements on peace process and national crisis while negotiations are in progress
1990 /91	Three meetings held in San José, Mexico, New York	Nine Accords reached concerning: Armed Forces; civil police; judicial system; electoral System; economic and social issues; political participation of FMLN; cease-fire; UN verification of accords; transition schedule	CPDN not recognised as representing civil society by government, although FMLN adopts some of the CPDN's proposals, all of which were published in paid newspaper ads
1992	Peace Accord signed in Mexico	Signing of Peace Accords marks the beginning of the demobilisation process and implementation of Accords. Operational agreements were made over the next two years to agree various necessary re-schedulings	

GUATEMALA

Background

The war in Guatemala was the longest-standing in Latin America. The first attempt to establish a guerrilla army was in March 1962, and Guatemala was the last Central American country to reach a peace accord — a decade after the idea of a negotiated settlement had begun to take shape. The formal negotiation process between the four organisations which formed the Guatemalan National Revolutionary Unity (URNG) and the government of Guatemala reached its final phase in December 1996, after unprecedently rapid advances in the months leading up to this. These advances were made possible by the new government's approach, as well as by the URNG's wish finally to participate in the political arena. Although formal negotiations took place between the two parties seated at the negotiating table, various sectors of civil society also exerted considerable influence. The global context, and international pressure on both sides to put an end to the armed conflict, were decisive.

Why was this armed conflict so particularly complex? As elsewhere in Central America, its origins lay in conditions of profound inequality and social and economic exclusion. But apart from the concentration of wealth in a few hands, while most people lacked access to basic resources, the indigenous indian majority suffered enormous discrimination. Successive governments had resorted to force rather than negotiation as a means of containing social conflicts. By consolidating a predominantly *ladino* [mixed blood, Spanish-speaking and often claiming Spanish descent — translator's note] culture that denied the country's ethnic diversity, successive regimes had essentially imposed a sense of national unity which was based upon an authoritarian and exclusive state. Thus, profound social and political contradictions had evolved over generations, mainly concerning the question of access to resources. Guatemala's social divisions were also marked by deeply entrenched forms of racism which permeated every aspect of society, and which are only now beginning to be debated more openly.

In addition, society had lived through over 30 years of armed conflict, and had established many defence-mechanisms. These very mechanisms fed the culture of terror which in turn closed off all outlets for frustration, or opportunities to develop consensus-based proposals for change. It is impossible to conceive of the true consequences of the war in Guatemala. The very nature of the government's counter-insurgency effort meant that the war was waged not only against the armed opposition, but was largely focused on people who were poor, on indigenous indian communities, on intellectuals and opposition leaders. The human injury was immense: some 100,000 people killed between 1954 and 1983, about 90,000 people 'disappeared', over 50,000 widows, 250,000 orphans, and over 440 villages obliterated from the face of the earth. The forms of torture and cruelty that many people experienced defy description. It was against this background that the two sides agreed to negotiate; and it is with this experience behind them that the more moderate and democratic elements of Guatemalan society now hope to build a new nation.

Why armed conflict? Essentially, Guatemala's social and economic structures had provoked repeated conflicts over the years, while also closing down any space for political participation. The resulting widespread discontent was the seed for armed conflict. Some analysts maintain that the frustrated democratic process marking the 1944–54 period, which ended with the coup d'état that ousted President Arbenz, tipped the balance in terms of social discontent. As democratic expression through peaceful means was denied, some social sectors grew increasingly radical. The key role of the US government in engineering the coup d'état gave the whole process a marked ideological character: both the internal opposition to President Arbenz and the US government presented his overthrow as part of the crusade against Communism within the cold-war context. Hence, Guatemala also became the launching-pad for attacks on Communism elsewhere in Latin America after Fidel Castro had taken power in Cuba; another factor which marked the Guatemalan revolutionary movement.

Today, like other countries in Central America, Guatemala faces a strategic dilemma in terms of how to address the needs of the poor majority in the process of transition towards peace. Economic globalisation tends to hold back the poorest countries from realising the benefits of wealth and production. Yet recent governments have adopted the neo-liberal model along with economic structural adjustment, believing that this is consistent with democratisation and dialogue. Central to this is the government's clear wish to subordinate the military to civilian authority (in a country in which military impunity remains a critical problem) while at the same time deepening its alliances with the more modernising tendencies within the military.

The negotiation process must be seen within this context. The impact of the neo-liberal economic model, which inherently tends to exclude the majority, can be softened only if the government is clearly committed to adopting redistributive policies. Moreover, if peace is to work, the more powerful sectors of Guatemalan society must be prepared to share some of the benefits that they enjoy with a population for whom the negotiated settlement will mean very little unless it is accompanied by improvements in material well-being and by increased opportunities to express and release their long-contained energies. The real resolution of the conflict and the construction of a sustainable peace in Guatemala need more than a general willingness to support the transition process. These developments will depend on Guatemalans' willingness to transform their attitudes, in a country which is perhaps the most politically and socially polarised in the region.

The peace negotiation process

Creating the conditions for talks

Two events created the conditions for promoting peace negotiations with the URNG: the Esquipulas II process and the international pressure that accompanied it, and the election in 1986 of the first civilian president in 15 years, leader of the Christian Democrat party, Vinicio Cerezo. At the start of the Cerezo government, the URNG announced its willingness not to stand in the way of any genuine democratic process and suspended its military offensives for several months, at the same time putting forward demands, meeting which would demonstrate the

government's commitment. The URNG then proposed a dialogue, to which the Cerezo government and the military responded by arguing that the guerrillas should first lay down their arms, claiming that the establishment of a civilian government inherently invalidated the armed struggle. Indeed, they even called for the guerrilla organisations to disband, a demand which the latter rejected on the grounds that the resolution of the conflict had to be based on negotiations on how to address its underlying causes. This issue repeatedly proved to be the stumbling block to any dialogue. Face-to-face meetings between both sides did not take place until 1987 — almost two years after the initial efforts had been made. However, the talks simply underlined their differences. In reality, the much-vaunted democracy of the Cerezo Administration was never more than a formal exercise. No steps were ever taken to demilitarise the country, or to dismantle the apparatus of state repression; nor were there any serious proposals to transform the unequal economic or social structures.

The Esquipulas II Accords which led to the establishment of National Reconciliation Commissions (CNRs) were fundamental in guaranteeing that Guatemalan civil society would in future be able to participate more actively. However, neither the Amnesty Decree 71–87 nor the formal establishment of the Commission were enough in themselves to ensure such participation at this stage. Rather, they served to expose the divergence between those who favoured negotiation (including the popular organisations) and those who opposed it (particularly the private sector and certain political parties). The Armed Forces were also divided over whether the government should negotiate with the URNG, so that it became still more difficult for civil-society organisations to reach a broad-based consensus and to put forward concrete proposals. Fear also served to limit wider participation.

The CNR comprised representatives from four social sectors: the government (the Vice-President and one other), the Catholic Church (the President of the Episcopal Conference, Mons. Quezada Toruño and Mons. Juan Gerardi [7]), 'respected citizens' (Teresa de Zarco and Licendiado Mario Permuth), and political parties (represented by Jorge Serrano, who would later become president of Guatemala, and Col Francisco Luis Gordillo). In 1987 and 1988, there were two exploratory meetings between the CNR and the URNG to set down the framework for subsequent negotiation. The CNR then embarked on dialogue with the URNG, with the support of the government (which asked to be informed of the outcomes).

In early 1988, the Episcopal Conference had published a letter entitled 'The Cry for Land' in which it stated that the need for peace must be linked with the much-needed resolution of the country's social problems. Along with other initiatives, this served to generate greater interest and participation in the nascent peace process within certain sectors. And although the URNG had received no response to its own call for National Dialogue, the two bishops who were members of the CNR decided to try to get this idea off the ground.

Thus, in November 1988, the CNR called on the government and civil-society organisations to participate in the National Dialogue that was to open the doors to broader social participation in subsequent debates. The Dialogue was inaugurated in February 1989 and continued until November 1990. Some 47 organisations partic-ipated — popular organisations, journalists, co-operatives, church and lay workers, the private sector, and the government. From the outset, the most significant absences were those of the Co-ordinating Committee of Agricultural, Commercial, Industrial, and Financial Associations (CACIF) and the National Agricultural Union (UNAGRO). These two bodies — the country's economic power-houses — argued that the National Debate was subject to political manip-ulation and questioned whether it was representative of Guatemalan society. In fact, they were unwilling to discuss changing any aspect of Guatemala's socio-economic structure that might negatively affect their interests.

The Dialogue did not deliver any concrete proposals to take to the negotiating table, but it did facilitate a series of social agreements which illustrated a broad consensus on the country's essential problems. These agreements established the framework for subsequent stages in the process. The government and the URNG did not, however, achieve significant progress in their negotiations: both sides continued to publish separate communiqués restating their respective positions.

Structuring the agenda and finding mechanisms for negotiation

In February 1990, President Cerezo created the post of Conciliator, who was the government's representative in the CNR, and called for a meeting in Oslo between the CNR and the URNG to prepare the conditions for direct dialogue. This marked the start of a dynamic that went beyond the framework of the Esquipulas II Accord. The resulting Oslo Accord marked the first concrete achievement in the peace process, although neither side was represented by its top negotiators. It was agreed to establish a series of meetings and dialogues between the URNG and various civil-society organisations (academics and business-people were also involved at a later stage); to commence meetings between the government and the URNG, to be witnessed by the CNR; and to request the UN to observe and guarantee compliance with what was agreed.

It still appears paradoxical that this Accord should have been signed by the URNG and representatives of Guatemalan civil society who enjoyed 'the government's complete support'. This can only be explained by the level of distrust and polarisation between the two opposing sides, which meant that civil society — especially the Catholic Church — came to be both mediator and signatory to an Accord that in turn helped to propel forward the entire negotiation process. Indeed, it led to real dialogue and civil-society participation, because, with the government's full knowledge and agreement, a series of talks and meetings then started between the URNG and various sectors of society. These resulted in the 1990 El Escorial Accord, which outlined the conditions for the URNG to participate in the process leading to the 1991 Constituent Assembly on the undertaking that it would not interfere with the elections. Another agreement reached in 1990, the Quito Declaration, was jointly signed by religious leaders and the URNG, the former stressing the importance of broad-based social participation and constitutional reform. The 1990 Metepec (Puebla) Declaration, signed with representatives of popular organisations and trade unions, raised the issue of human rights, and the rights of indigenous indians. The 1990 Atlixco Declaration, signed with representatives of civil society and the business sector (with the exception of CACIF, which refused to participate), emphasised the need for peaceful solutions to the conflict and the need for comprehensive participation in this process. Only the bilateral meeting with CACIF, held in Ottawa, did not yield positive results. Instead, each side issued its own communiqué: the URNG stressed the importance of having met, and CACIF emphasised the damage caused by the conflict and its differences with the URNG, but also stated its willingness to seek legally acceptable solutions.

This round of meetings with the URNG was to lay the foundations for the subsequent involvement of civil-society organisations in the peace process. While this did not become a nationwide participation — either in terms of the scope of the discussion nor in terms of representation — it was nevertheless important in opening the space for discussion on the process itself, and also in encouraging an expression of public opinion, in a society that had until then been marginalised in the political debate. Although the meetings failed to produce concrete agreements (hardly to be expected in the circumstances), they did mark the beginning of efforts to build a consensus around peace and democracy. Marked ideological differences existed between those who were hostile to, and those who sympathised with, the URNG, and parties disagreed on whether there was a need for structural transformation, but everyone recognised the need for institutional and constitutional changes, respect for human rights, a genuine and participatory democracy, and for direct dialogue between the URNG, the government, and the military.

The indigenous indian (or Mayan) sector was conspicuous by its absence from these meetings, which participated along with the other popular sectors rather than as a separate group. Given that people of Mayan descent represent the majority of the Guatemalan population, their specific demands clearly needed to be expressed and addressed in their own right. The negotiation process and the initiatives of certain leaders did later open up important spaces for the Mayan indians, unprecendented in Guatemala's recent history. Women too were later to participate as a social sector within the Civil Society Assembly.

The political struggle and the start of negotiations

During the following months, the Army reiterated that the guerrillas must lay down their arms and return to public life before negotiations could progress. In October 1990, the Minister of Defence stressed that the Army was 'inflexible' in its view that the government should only enter into dialogue with the URNG if it first disarmed, regardless of any other dialogues underway between the URNG and other social sectors. The URNG, however, insisted on distinguishing between substantive issues for negotiation and the operational aspects, such as demobilisation, which could only be defined once agreement had been reached on the fundamental points.

The latter part of 1990 saw a rise in the incidence of kidnappings, 'disappearances', or politically motivated killings. The year ended with a massacre of *campesinos* in Santiago Atitlán, which happened in the middle of the electoral campaign which brought to power Jorge Serrano Elías. Over the next few months, President Serrano spoke of the need to reach a total peace agreement, but failed to respond to the proposals for direct meetings which the UNRG was making.

Initially, Serrano said that he would be willing in principle to negotiate directly with the URNG. These talks would have to be private and brief. The URNG also expressed its desire for peace, but insisted on the need for political agreements as well as practical arrangements, including verification. This period was marked by a constant 'stretching and shrinking', as each side in turn hardened and softened its position, depending on how much national and international support they felt they had at any given time. The URNG stepped up its military activities, while the Serrano government announced on 8 April 1991 its 'Initiative for Total Peace'. This initiative, however, ignored the advances that had already been made in the Oslo Accord, focusing solely on the question of dismantling the guerrilla forces. While the URNG rejected this proposal, it finally agreed to its first direct meeting with the government and the Army.

On 26 April 1991, this encounter finally took place in Mexico City. The government delegation included five high-ranking military officials, and the URNG was represented by its High Command. The 'Accord on Procedures for the Search for Peace through Political Means' was signed, in which each side committed itself to 'achieving a negotiation process that would, within the shortest time possible, lead to the signing of a firm and lasting peace, based on political accords and agreeements on their implementation, and outlining the terms on which compliance would be verified by the National Reconciliation Commission (CNR), the United Nations Organisation (UN), and other international bodies by mutual agreement'. The agenda items for subsequent meetings were also agreed, and included the following points:

- democratisation and human rights;
- strengthening civil power and defining the role of the military within a democractic society;
- the identity and rights of indigenous peoples;
- constitutional reform and the electoral system;
- socio-economic aspects;
- the agrarian situation,
- resettlement of populations displaced by the armed conflict;
- preparations for the URNG to enter national political life;
- arrangements for a definitive cease-fire;
- a timetable for implementing and verifying compliance with the Accords,
- signing an Accord for Firm and Lasting Peace, and demobilisation.

This was significant not only because it set out the negotiation agenda, but also because it dealt with all the substantive issues that had arisen in the course of the process of National Dialogue. Yet although this Accord opened up new opportunities for discussion and showed greater flexibility than had been the case, the negotiations became deadlocked on the first issue: democratisation. It took the two parties two meetings, held in the Mexican cities of Cuernavaca and Querétaro in June and July 1991, for both parties to agree on what democratisation meant. The so-called Querétaro Accord provided a general framework for establishing a shared concept of what democratisation should entail within the political, economic, social, and cultural spheres, with a focus on the rights of every Guatemalan citizen. In formal terms at least, this Accord marked an historic advance in the democratisation process. The document recognised the preeminence of civil society, and accepted that the Armed Forces should be subject to civil authority in order to establish a state of law.

The negotiation process stumbles

The question of human rights was the next item on the agenda. Given the country's history and, in particular, the role of the Armed Forces, this was to be one of the most difficult and complex issues. The serious differences between the various parties, reflecting Guatemala's profoundly polarised society, meant that the process stalled. The publication of the 'Accord on the Civil Defence Patrols' in August 1991, which included certain points on the democratisation process, was roundly criticised by the military and the private sector. At the same time, there was a rise in the incidence of human-rights violations by the government and the Army. The URNG consequently received greater international support for its position, which in turn led to a hardening in the government's line, and an emphasis on military issues.

In May 1992, the URNG launched its proposal 'Guatemala: a Just and Democratic Peace — The Contents of Negotiation', in which it pronounced on the 'substantive issues' – points which it considered indispensable — of the Mexico Accord. In a U-turn on its earlier insistence that the URNG guerrillas demobilise as a pre-condition for negotiations, the government now proposed resuming discussions on human rights.

Against this backdrop, CACIF and the AGA publicly accused the URNG of being responsible for Guatemala's problems, calling on it to surrender, and expressing their disagreement even with the idea of discussing the substantive issues. In contrast, the organisations which had participated in the National Dialogue demanded that they should also participate in the negotiation process, and reiterated the importance of the substantive issues.

However, in January 1993 President Serrano proposed a 'Peace Plan' that called for a URNG cease-fire without having even reached agreement on the substantive issues. Simultaneously, the Army began a major military offensive. The URNG maintained that it would negotiate only on the substantive issues. Thus, negotiations had virtually broken down by May 1993; and neither side had achieved its goals. While there had been some partial pre-accords, the attempts to address the substantive issues had demonstrated deep divisions, especially over the establishment of a Truth Commission to investigate past human-rights violations, and over international verfication of compliance with the Accords.

After almost two years, and several rounds of negotiations since the first Accord was supposed to have been formalised, the Accord on Human Rights had still not been signed when Serrano engineered a coup d'état on 25 May 1993. Various social groupings had mobilised during the negotiation process, particularly in the capital, where important student, teacher, and popular organisations protested against the worsening socio-economic situation. Many of their demands were more radical than those of the URNG. The dynamic that had been generated by the negotiations, and the need for the government to hold this in check, were probably the main reasons behind the decision of Serrano and the Army to fabricate a coup d'état (although the Army was at first opposed to the idea).

This attempt failed, and opposition within Guatemala was in fact backed up by strong international condemnation and even by the Guatemalan business sector. The Army then retracted and brought down Serrano. Amid widespread popular support, Ramiro de León Carpio (then the Human Rights Procurator) was installed as president on 6 June 1993.

De León's candidature was proposed to the Congress by the National Consensus Body created in the wake of the Serrano affair. Although it existed for only a few months, it became an unprecedented forum for reaching broad-based consensus (including CACIF). This experience proved significant in encouraging the subsequent participation of civil-society organisations in the peace-negotiation process, and also influenced the eventual proposals to purge the state apparatus.

Expectations were high that de León's government would actively resume the peace negotiation process. The response of democratic and civil-society organisations to the fake coup had also shown the extent of people's wish to break with the governing powers' traditional intransigence and to create new forms of participation. However, the affair also allowed the Army to turn around its international image to take on the role of guarantor of democracy. This had further repercussions, because certain sectors within the Army realised that it was possible to confront the national crisis in a relatively open way.

Immediately after de León became president, the URNG proposed to meet with him. Various parts of civil society also urged him to resume negotiations, based on what exisiting agreements, and to make them as participatory as possible. To the surprise of many, de León claimed that the peace discussions were not his immediate priority, and that before resuming negotiations his government would review what had gone before. From the outset, however, the focus was on questions concerning the modernisation and restructuring of the state apparatus, the democratisation of political parties, and other substantive issues.

In July 1993, the president and his adviser, Hector Rosada, presented a 'Proposal to Resume the Peace Process'. This revolved around two focal points. First, a Permanent Peace Forum comprising representatives of various social sectors, including the URNG (with Mons. Quezada y Toruño as its president). Ist main aim would be to foster agreement in relation to the Substantive Issues. However, these agreements would *not* represent government commitments; and the URNG could participate in the Forum only if it first laid down arms. The second point was that negotiations between the government and the URNG would be mediated by a commission made up of representatives of the UN and the OAS. This would discuss operational matters concerning demobilisation of the guerrilla forces. Simultaneously, the CNR was dissolved, and a Government Peace Commission (COPAZ) was set up, headed by Rosada. In essence, this proposal would marginalise Mons. Quezada y Toruño from moderating the negotiations.

The URNG stated that it would participate in the Forum if its security were guaranteed, but pointed out serious gaps and flaws in the proposal: it wiped out three years of negotiations which had already gained some achievements and failed to recognise all the parties in the process. Third, it changed the orginal role of the conciliator. The URNG insisted on holding a preliminary meeting with a government-Army delegation, to be presided over by Mons. Quezada y Toruño, in order to agree on the points on which negotiations could resume.

Civil-society organisations regarded the government proposal as inadquate, arguing that to separate the substantive issues from operational matters was a backwards step. They also stressed the need to take existing accords into account, to respect the agenda items already been agreed, and to recognise the progress made during the National Dialogue meetings in 1990. However, the private sector opposed URNG participation in the Forum, and its leading representatives rejected even the idea of negotiating with the URNG, arguing that it was unconstitutional to enter into discussion with an outlawed body. The Minister of Defence openly opposed any possible Truth Commission. The result was that de León's proposal achieved no concrete results; in August 1993 the URNG expressed disappointment that the government had failed to make any progress because of the recalcitrance of the private sector and the Army.

At the same time, international pressure (from UN, the OAS, and certain governments) regarding the human-rights situation and the need to reach a Peace Accord increased. Some individuals within the IMF and the World Bank also made declarations to the same effect, motivated in part by their concern to ensure that the Guatemalan government comply with its financial commitments and create a stable climate which would encourage investment.

In September 1993, the government appointed a new peace commission made up of three military officers and three civilians, under the leadership of Hector Rosada. Earlier that month, the Minister of Defence also announced a major military offensive against the guerrilla forces, and Mons. Quezada y Toruño released the 'pre-project for the resumption of peace talks' that had already been presented to the parties concerned. This was widely judged a considered and impartial document, and was generally accepted by popular groups. The URNG also pronounced itself in favour, though this was questioned by the government. On 24 September, the government's peace commission, COPAZ, also announced its peace plan, which was presented to the President and the Military High Command. The Minister of Defence declared that he was satisfied with this plan, which de León then presented first to the diplomatic community and then to the Guatemalan public. It had three main components:

• The Permanent Peace Forum would be developed nation-wide, as a means of analysing the country's problems and finding solutions. The Forum would be convened by the CNR. The URNG would not participate directly, but could submit its views through the CNR.

• The government promised to respond to social demands and to strengthen respect for human rights.

• The government and Army would negotiate with the URNG about a definitive cease-fire and the latter's return to legality by means of an amnesty, after which it would be permitted to participate in the Permanent Forum. A representative of the UN Secretary-General would convene, advise, and moderate the negotiations, and verify certain operational aspects.

In addition, the government made an 'Official Declaration on Human Rights', committing itself to guarantee these in a way that implicitly replaced the Global Accord on Human Rights, which had been under negotiation for almost two years.

The URNG leadership rejected the Rosada plan, arguing that it both altered the spirit of and impeded the negotiation process, and in fact denied the URNG's status as a party within this process. However, it agreed to meet with COPAZ, in the presence of the conciliator and the UN observer, in order to agree the basic conditions for resuming negotiations. Its point of departure would be the proposals put forward by the conciliator, with a view to signing the Global Accord on Human Rights. The Army — with the President's backing – responded by threatening to by-pass the URNG leadership and negotiate directly with the rank-and-file combatants. This threat never materialised. Rather, the URNG reiterated that it would remain faithful to the Oslo Accord by first negotiating and reaching political agreement on the substantive issues, and only then proceeding to negotiate operational questions such as the cease-fire, demobilisation, and a return to political life.

Many civil-society organisations and local people regarded the Rosada plan as a re-hashed version of what the previous government had proposed, and argued that it did not reflect the hopes of the Guatemalan people. Their rejection was based on the fact that the plan back-tracked on negotiated agreements; that it failed to address the country's problems since it separated the causes of the conflict from the peace process; that it negated the Human Rights Accord and eliminated the role of international verification, for instance through the Truth Commission; and that the functioning of the Permanent Peace Forum remained unclear, as did the decision-making capacity of civil-society organisations, especially since the role of conciliator no longer existed. They also underlined that peace meant more than a cease-fire, and claimed that the Rosada plan was unviable. Instead, they supported the proposals of Mons. Quezada y Toruño. The Episcopal Conference likewise insisted on honouring the Oslo and Mexico Accords in relation to the procedures and agenda for negotiations, describing the government plan as 'infeasible'.

In spite of the government's real efforts to gather international backing for its plan, very few countries offered explicit support, although many declared that they favoured peace negotiations. The UN Secretary-General concurred with this position, while the EU went further and suggested that the government revise its plan to accommodate those areas of consensus within Guatemalan society.

Yet despite this widespread rejection, the COPAZ co-ordinator announced that in January

1994 the Forum would begin its work. As a first step, the former CNR would re-convene, and steps would be taken to enable Guatemalan society to participate. But it was widely considered that the re-convening of a new CNR both ignored and displaced the role of Mons. Quezada y Toruño as conciliator. Having now been excluded from any role in the negotiation process, the Episcopal Conference, and Mons. Quezada y Toruño in particular, opted to stay out of the CNR. Certain government officials spoke in similar tones, arguing that peace was more than the absence of war, and that the resolution of the conflict needed to go hand-in-hand with a solution to the underlying causes. By mid-December 1993, the Procurator for Human Rights was accusing the de León government of being responsible for the breakdown in negotiations.

In November 1993, the first of a series of Ecumenical Conferences for Peace in Guatemala, organised by the Lutheran World Federation (LWF) and the World Council of Churches (WCC), was held in Washington DC. The conflicting parties and various representatives of Guatemalan civil society were invited, as well as members of the international community. Although they were subsequently sto change their position, neither the government, the Army, nor the Guatemalan private sector agreed to participate, claiming that they were not prepared to be treated on equal terms with the URNG. The Conference called for a resumption of direct talks between the government and the URNG.

After this, the URNG High Command and its political and diplomatic team were invited to New York by the UN Secretary-General. The URNG stated its willingness to participate in a preliminary meeting, to be convened by the UN Secretary-General and attended by Mons. Quezada y Toruña, which would establish the framework for a negotiation process. This whole phase was embarked upon against a backdrop of growing international pressure for peace which was eventually to open up new channels of negotiation and allow for greater popular participation.

The peace-negotiation process resumes

In December 1993, a UN spokesperson announced that the Guatemalan government and the URNG had agreed to meet in Mexico City on 9 January 1994. This meeting was aimed at 'reaching a joint definition of the terms on which the negotiation process would be resumed'. The Framework Accord for the Resumption of the Negotiation Process of January 1994 outlined the following steps:

• The parties in conflict would negotiate on all the items outlined in the 1991 Mexico Accord, and compliance with all the undertakings would be subject to verification.

• The UN Secretary-General would be asked to appoint a moderator, who would propose initiatives to foster the signing of an agreement for firm and lasting peace.

• An Assembly would be set up which would be open to participation by all non-government sectors, who would discuss the substantive issues, make recommendations to the negotiators, and support the agreements reached in order to ensure that these became nation-wide under-takings.

• The Guatemalan Episcopal Conference would be asked to delegate one of its members as president of this Assembly; the Accord suggested that Mons. Quezada y Toruño was well qualified for this role. The president would be supported by an organising committee made up of representatives from a cross-section of society, and would be responsible for convening and managing the Assembly's deliberations, acting as a bridge between this and the parties at the negotiating table, and being allowed to participate in special sessions.

• The governments of Colombia, Mexico, Norway, Spain, the USA, and Venezuela would be asked to form a Group of Friends of the peace process, in order to support the UN's role and strengthen the commitments undertaken by the parties in conflict, acting as witnesses of honour to the accords reached.

This Framework Accord represented a return to the earlier course of negotiation, and guaranteed broad-based participation through the Assembly. The conciliator would be replaced by a UN-appointed Moderator, Jean Arnaud.

The Global Accord on Human Rights was signed in Mexico City on 29 March 1994. It was the first Accord which acknowledged the significance of the substantive issues in achieving an end to armed conflict. It came into immediate effect. The UN Verification Mission (MINUGUA) was to be in charge of verification, although this body was not established for some time. MINUGUA was also mandated to receive denunciations of human-rights violations and ensure that these were adequately handled by the judicial system, as well as making any recommendations deemed necessary. A further role was to make efforts to strengthen the capacity of any government and non-government organisations concerned with protecting human rights.

The 1994 Accord established the government's responsibility for ensuring full respect for human rights, challenging impunity for offences committed, offering guarantees for civil protection, dismantling clandestine or illegal structures, and ensuring freedom of association and movement. The government also agreed to offer special support to the victims of human-rights violations, and to strengthen human-rights organisations. The URNG undertook to respect human rights; and both sides made special reference to the rights of casualties and prisoners of war.

A new negotiating timetable was also agreed. While this was not followed to the letter (a contingency provided for within the Accord on the Timetable of Negotiations for a Firm and Lasting Peace in Guatemala), it nevertheless offered a framework for the Assembly to put forward proposals. Although such proposals were not binding, they offered civil-society organisations a way of making their views known to both parties. The intention was to reach agreement within eight months on all the substantive issues already identified, with the definitive Peace Accord and demobilisation scheduled for December 1994. The Moderator would fix the dates for each round of negotiation, as well as the Special Sessions which would permit any 'recommendations or orientations' to be transmitted from the Assembly to the negotiators. In practice, the combination of political interests and attempts to reach alliances, both inside Guatemala and internationally, all prolonged the process, to the extent that negotiations were not concluded until the end of 1996.

Steps forward: various Accords

The Accord on the Resettlement of Populations Displaced by the Armed Conflict was signed in June 1994, representing an attempt to solve the problems faced by the civilian population most affected by the armed conflict. It set out a strategy for resettling the displaced in which the government agreed to consult fully with the affected population. It was proposed to establish a six-person joint commission, to be made up of two representatives each from the government and the displaced population, and two advisers from international aid agencies. The commission's mandate was to draw up projects that responded to the needs and interests of the displaced. In addition, both signatories asked UNESCO to assist in designing a plan to support educational activities among this population, and requested that any funds for projects arising from this Accord be administered by UNDP.

The strategy was to focus on fighting poverty and to guarantee the rights of the displaced, assuring their political, social, and economic reintegration, in the wider context of seeking sustainable and equitable development in Guatemala, and promoting reconciliation efforts within the resettlement areas. The Accord emphasised the need to protect the rights of the Mayan population in general, and of women-headed households in particular. It also addressed the need to clear the main areas of fighting of mines and explosives. The government committed itself to recognising formal and informal studies of this population, and facilitating access to legal documents for the displaced and any children born outside the country, as well as guaranteeing their land rights (including possession and use).

The Accord on Establishing a Commission for the Historic Clarification of Human Rights Violations and Acts of Violence that had caused Suffering to the Guatemalan Population was signed in Oslo in June 1994. This provided for a Commission to be set up by the UN Moderator, who would nominate a person of irreproachable reputation, acceptable to both parties; and select a scholar from candidates put forward by the universities. This Commission would become effective six months from the date of signing the Firm and Lasting Peace Accord (with the possibility of a six-month extension). The Commission would act discreetly and not disclose its sources of information, in order to guarantee witnesses' security. Its mandate was to clarify human-rights violations and acts of violence committed from the start of the armed conflict until the final Accord, and to make recommendations for strengthening the democratisation process and preserving the memory of the victims, to move towards a culture of peace and respect. The Accord did not contemplate identifying individual respon-sibility for any such acts; it left this decision to the citizens of Guatemala. Given the history of impunity for human-rights violations, this was highly controversial.

The Accord on the Identity and Rights of the Indigenous Peoples signed in Mexico in March

1995 was singularly important, given Guatemala's history and the fact that its population is mostly Mayan. The Accord (summarised in Appendix 2) acknowledged that Guatemala is a multi-ethnic, multi-cultural, and multi-lingual nation, and that the indigenous indian population had suffered particularly from discrimination, exploitation, and injustice. The Accord covered matters including constitutional reforms, ethnic discrimination, sexual harassment, cultural rights and spiritual values (including education), amd the necessary legal and institutional reforms to guarantee the full civil, political, social, and economic rights of the indigenous peoples. It recognised the Co-ordinating Body of the Organisations of the Guatemalan Mayan People (COPMAGUA) as the representative body of the Mayan, Garifuna, and Xinca communities, and established five commissions charged with taking forward relevant proposals. Of these, three were to be joint — the Commissions on Educational Reform, on Reform and Political Participation, and on Land-related Rights of the Indian Peoples. The remaining two — on the Official Status of Indigenous Languages and on Defining and Preserving Sacred Places — were not designed as joint commissions.

Although talks had begun with the de León government on the question of socio-economic development and the agrarian situation, concrete progress was only made with the incoming government of Alvaro Arzú in May 1996. The new government heralded changes in the tone and dynamic of the negotiations: both parties expressed themselves satisfied with 'the climate of trust' between them. The Accord on Socio-Economic Aspects and the Agrarian Situation (see Appendix 2) stressed that social justice was the basis for the socio-economic development and national unity of Guatemala. It covered issues concerning democratisation and participatory development, through the establishment of rural development councils; social development and changes in public-spending priorities, and programmes to favour health and education; agrarian reform, which covered land use and tenure as well as credit, technical assistance, and protection of natural resources; and the modernisation of the fiscal system in order to increase tax revenue and clamp down on fraud and evasion. It was to come into effect as soon as the final Accord was signed, although the government committed itself to start the necessary planning immediately.

The Accord on the Strengthening of Civil Power and the Role of the Army within a Democratic Society was signed in Mexico City in September 1996 and concluded the negotiations on the substantive issues. It dealt with aspects ranging from the definition and reform of public institutions such as the legislature, the judiciary and justice system, the role of the executive and the subordination of the military and state security forces to civilian rule; the participation of women and other marginalised parts of society; and the question of disarmament, demilitarisation of the social fabric, and massive demobilisation. It also provided for the disbanding of the so-called Voluntary Civil Defence Committees (or Civil Patrols), which were set up by the Armed Forces in the 1980s as a means of making rural communities in the indian highlands responsible for 'policing' the counter-insurgency effort. (See Appendix 2.)

With these accords, the negotiation round on the substantive issues was concluded, and a rapid round of negotiations on the 'operational issues' began. The Accord on the Definitive Cease-fire was signed in Oslo on 4 December 1996, which related to the gathering of the URNG forces, their disarmament and subsequent demobilisation. The Accord on Constitutional and Electoral Reforms was signed in Stockholm on 7 December 1996, and requested Congress to detail and enact the consititutional reforms required to implement each of the substantive accords. The Accord on Legalising the Guatemalan National Revolutionary Unity (URNG) was signed in Madrid five days later, covering the conditions and formal provisions which would allow the URNG to become a legal entity. Finally, the Accord on the Timetable for Implementing, Fulfilling, and Verifying the Peace Accords was signed in Guatemala on 29 December 1996, on the same day as the Accord on Firm and Lasting Peace was finalised. This outlined the timetable to guide the implementation of all the commitments and undertakings contained in the various Peace Accords, including a schedule for those aspects that did not include general or permanent provisions. This accord also established an Accompaniment Commission to act as a political and technical reference point for the Technical Secretariat of the Peace Process. This would be formed in January 1997 with representatives from both sides, four citizens of their choice, one member of Congress, and the head of the UN international verification mission (with observer status only).

The Accord on Firm and Lasting Peace was signed in Guatemala City on 29 December 1996 in a ceremony conducted at the National Palace and attended by members of the URNG, the government, the Army, and special guests from Guatemala and the international community, as well as the UN Moderators and representatives of friendly countries. The moment was also marked by celebrations throughout the country, and a mass demonstration in the central square attended by hundreds of Guatemalan organisations and individuals.

Table 3: Chronology of peace negotiations in Guatemala

Year	Event	Results	Civil-society participation
First phase			
1986	Declaration of Intent	Publication of respective positions in media	
1987	Esquipulas II Declaration of Procedures to establish Firm and Lasting Peace in Central America	Accord signed at Presidential Summit; National Reconciliation Commissions established	
Second phase			
1987	1st meeting (low-level) between government and URNG	No agreement	CNR formed
1988	First and second meeting between CNR-URNG	No accord, but possibility of meeting between URNG and government	
	CNR calls for National Dialogue between government and civil-society organisations	Sounding out of URNG intentions on peace; no result.	
1989/ 90	National Dialogue commences March and concludes in November 1990	Social agreements show wide consensus. Mons. Quezada named as Conciliator and government representative	
Oslo Accord			
	Basic Accord to seek peace between CNR (with government backing) and URNG	Oslo Accord and first concrete achievement. Mechanisms to meet with various social and economic sectors established as part of National Dialogue.	
	Direct talks between government and URNG high command	Escorial, Quito, Metepec and Atlixco Declarations signed. Two communiqués from Otlanar (meetings with CACIF)	
First sub-phase			
	Government peace initiative rejected by URNG, but first meeting agreed.	Mexico Accord signed	International community with reduced influence
	Accord on proceedings for peace negotiations		Mons. Quezada plays leading role
	Accord on Democratisation	Querétaro Accord signed	Various pronouncements by civil society (popular sector, parties, and private sector)
	Agreements on Human Rights		
1991/ 92	URNG issues peace proposal Partial Accords published	Government proposes to return to human-rights issue	
1993	Government Peace Plan (for cease-fire) Other meetings	URNG insists on dealing with substantive issues No progress	

Table 3: Chronology of peace negotiations in Guatemala *continued*

Year	Event	Results	Civil-society participation
Second sub-phase			
	New government proposes resumption of peace process	Proposal widely rejected, no advances in negotiation	
	Mons. Quezada presides over efforts to get process started	Quezada plan accepted by URNG and popular sectors, rejected by government	
	Government Peace Plan and Official Declaration on Human Rights	Rejected by URNG and civil-society organisations	
1994	Accord on resumption of peace talks signed by government, URNG and CNR	Accord on resumption of peace talks signed	Civil Society Assemby established
Third phase			
	Global Accord on Human Rights	Accords signed	
	Accord on schedule for talks		
	Accord on Persons and Populations Displaced by Armed Conflict		
	Accord on Commission for Historical Clarification of human-rights violations and other forms of violence	Human Rights Commission set up	
1995	Mexico Accord on Identity and Rights of Indigenous Peoples	Accord signed recognising multi-ethic, pluri-cultural, and multi-lingual nature of Guatemalan nation, and acknowledging the particular suffering inflicted on the indigenous peoples	
		COPMAGUA accepted as respresentative body of indian peoples	
1996	Accord on Socio-economic Aspects and Agrarian Situation	Negotiations speed up. Accord underlines social justice as basis for socio-economic development and national unity	
	Mexico Accord on Strengthening Civil Power and Function of Army in Democratic Society	Mexico Accord marks conclusion of substantive issues	
Operational Accords for Firm and Lasting Peace			
	Oslo: Definitive cease-fire	All Accords signed	
	Stockholm: Constitutional and Electoral Reform		
	Legalisation of URNG		
	Agreement on schedule for implementation and verification		
	Firm and Lasting Peace Accord		

Chapter Three: International NGOs in Central America

Introduction

If 'the original sin' that underlies conflict is unequal access to resources and participation both between the North and the South, and within countries, it follows that the growing gap between rich and poor sustains and may even aggravate such conflicts.

In Central America, economic structural adjustment policies (SAPs) have inflicted on the already poor majority the burden of rising unemployment, and reduced access to basic services (heightened by the growing privatisation of social welfare provision). Obviously, there is no mechanistic cause-and-effect connection between this and the possibility of renewed armed conflict in the region. However, the lack of perspectives and opportunities for the vast majority of the population — especially those elements of society who were most directly involved in the war and who thus became at least partly unsuited for civilian life — is leading to isolated cases of violence and to widespread social breakdown.

This chapter reflects on the complex problems and challenges which international aid agencies faced in working for peaceful solutions to the armed conflicts that ravaged Mexico and Central America in the 1980s. The aim is to identify elements that might be helpful in developing strategies for dealing with conflict and democratisation in this region and elsewhere.

The international co-operation that occurred in the region during the war years has not been well documented, especially during the worst periods of the conflicts. Various factors contributed to this:

• Conditions of insecurity in the region placed real constraints on what could be put in writing about the work that NGOs were supporting, and the ways in which they were doing so. Aid agency personnel and their local counterpart organisations faced real, and felt threatened by perceived, dangers.

• For the same reasons, many written reports went into great detail about what was happening at a global level, with far fewer specifics about individual country programmes.

• The series of emergencies in the region — major natural disasters in addition to the armed conflicts — were not addressed through operational programmes (which provide physical infrastructure) in the way that relief and development agencies traditionally work in other parts of the world. In Mexico and Central America, the immediate emergencies tended to be set in the context of the prevailing structural conditions, and linked with development support. Thus, with one or two exceptions [such as that of the 1985 earthquakes in Mexico or Hurricane Joan in Nicaragua two years later — translator's note] there was relatively little opportunity to bring the experience from the region to the head offices of the various aid agencies and NGOs.

• The institutional culture in many international aid agencies stresses 'rapid response' and immediate impact: thus there is relatively little investment in systematisation, reflection, and analysis of their own experience. This is aggravated by the pressure to raise funds, which is now increasingly defining the choice of programmes; and by the absence of any systems to develop an institutional memory or capture institutional history.

• Staff changes, which in general were not accompanied by appropriate handover periods, left major gaps in the institutional memory of certain agencies. These gaps were filled only partially and unsystematically, and the effort has meant considerable extra work for the incoming staff.

• The complex nature of the conflicts in Mexico and Central America, and the very language and style of communication used, posed huge challenges for those institutions and agencies whose background and history have tended to make it easier for them to interpret and engage with events in Africa or Asia than in Latin America. This may have been reinforced by the fact that the protagonists of the armed conflicts of Central America were struggling to make their own voices heard, using language that was relatively politicised and articulate. The challenge for the local offices of international agencies was to communicate with (*como instituciones interlocutoras*) their counterparts, not speak on their behalf.

• Many of the larger international agencies have for several years been absorbed in endless changes and re-structuring processes, but without the financial security to allow them to make medium- or long-term commitments. These re-structurings have made ever more demands on staff time, and distracted them from thinking about their programmes on the ground.

This chapter focuses on the most relevant aspects of the work of and the dilemmas faced by various international aid agencies in Mexico and Central America during the 1980s and early 1990s. While the conflicts were at their height at that time, many of the underlying problems remain; and conflicts continue today, although they are expressed in other ways and are finding new outlets.

Global picture of international aid in the region

By the late 1970s, several major aid agencies recognised that their support was principally directed towards assisting the victims of political violence and repression, and strengthening the capacity of social organisations to get their demands on to the national agenda. An increasing number of their counterparts were the victims of systematic threats or direct attacks on their work in promoting popular organisation, or activities which defended and educated people about human rights. This meant that the agencies' work was gradually shifting towards emergency programmes, even before the widespread outbreak of armed conflicts.

Throughout the 1980s and the early 1990s, any development work had to take place against the background of the region-wide conflict, within which each country had its own dynamics and characteristics. In response to the armed conflict, certain agencies had to modify their strategies and organisational structures, according to their existing knowledge and understanding of Central America, as well as existing relationships with their counterparts. All these factors influenced the evolution of their work.

Two basic criteria guided agencies' decisions about what work to support, and how to support it: first, the idea of supporting processes, and evaluating specific projects within this wider context; second, that of supporting groups with the potential to shape and influence social change. This meant that their programmes would not focus directly on 'the poorest of the poor', for although the kind of social transformation they envisaged would clearly benefit the poor majority, they sought to address the basic causes of poverty by strengthening the capacity of those who could best influence and change the structures which maintained poverty and injustice. Development assistance in this sense is based on strengthening people's organisational cacacity, to enable them to become agents of their own development.

Major events affecting NGO assistance in Central America

The 1979 overthrow of the Somoza dictatorship in Nicaragua created a climate of optimism among the revolutionary movements and popular groups in both Guatemala and El Salvador. Increases in their membership were countered with intense military repression, directed not only against the guerrilla organisations, but also against the popular movement — indeed, aginst any form of social organisation regarded as part of the opposition. In El Salvador and Guatemala, murders, 'disappearances', threats, and harassment of leaders of communities and organisations, and against the NGOs that supported them, became commonplace. Staff safety was in jeopardy. As a result, most of the international NGOs in the region moved their regional offices from the countries in which their programmes were largely based, to nearby countries such as Mexico or Costa Rica. This decision was the first major dilemma that these agencies were to face in the early 1980s.

This decision meant that support for emergency and development work had to be channeled through intermediary organisations, without actually having staff on the ground to monitor these projects first-hand. Gradually, it became possible to make short visits, although still at high personal risk. (Throughout most of the 1980s, the only country without such problems was Nicaragua, notwithstanding a few isolated problems there.)

What was the focus of NGO support?

'If we had known what was going to happen in Rwanda, perhaps we wouldn't have supported social organisation and group empowerment work in the same way'. The author's initial response to this comment by an international aid worker, was dissent. But this gave way to deeper reflections on the responsibility of international assistance in conflicts and potential conflicts, and about their particular understanding of power and its implications.

International aid agencies can be tremendously arrogant. What the comment on Rwanda seems to imply is that events there might have followed a different path had the agency in question not 'empowered' groups who, thanks to this support, took to violence in order to achieve their objectives. But the observation does have a certain validity. While international agencies cannot determine the direction in which a people proceeds, agencies' actions (or inaction) nevertheless affect the context within which such processes evolve; and this responsibility needs to be properly assumed.

In Central America, and more recently in Mexico, many international NGOs made a conscious commitment to stand by the poor and the marginalised, and to support those groups that could potentially bring about positive social change. In such highly polarised settings, this meant getting involved in the struggle to transform (or at least modify) the power relations between those with resources and those who had historically been denied them. This was evidently a political choice, even if support was given to non-combatant civilians who could develop organisational structures, and who were working to change the status quo. Empowerment was viewed, then, as the vehicle for transforming the poverty and exclusion in which most Central Americans were living; and organisations representing the poor would be the best way to bring about the kind of social transformation that would address the causes of poverty.

Thus, such agencies gave priority to supporting the establishment and consolidation of organisational structures which were able not only to channel resources and 'give voice' to the problems faced by poor people, but which could also become real actors in bringing about social transformation. This presupposed that they would mainly support intermediary or grassroots organisations, rather than assisting indviduals or groups who were not in some way linked into an organisational structure, or warvictims. It also meant that while their aim was to address poverty, the agencies did not work directly with the poorest of the poor, but with their leaders and intermediary organisations working alongside them.

Although international NGOs often worked with organisations that had emerged in response to the conflict, a common thread ran through their programmes in terms of how local counterparts were chosen. Essentially, they gave priority to those with whom they had worked before the conflicts became so acute. Personal trust necessarily plays a critical role in determining how an international aid agency functions in a context of political polarisation and armed conflict. In Central America, this level of trust with both individuals and groups took many years to build, and developed not only through a funding relationship, but also through a process of accompaniment and systematic discussions about their various problems and their strategies. This investment in the gradual process of trust-building eventually expanded the scope for contact with local people. It may also have reduced the high risk of errors that might have been politically costly for these agencies — always a real danger in the context of an armed conflict.

International NGO support was largely concentrated in two areas:

• 'Accompaniment' (direct physical accompaniment by agency staff or by third parties) from the onset of the emergency; and intensive lobbying to encourage inter-agency co-ordination in order to 'legitimise' the right of non-combatant civilians to receive humanitarian aid, irrespective of their political affinities.

• Provision of humanitarian aid through the churches, NGOs, and popular organisations, especially for civilian settlements in the conflict areas, both in order to help civilians survive and to strengthen their capacity to formulate their own demands and to become social actors and political protagonists in shaping the process of transformation.

Civil society in armed conflict

The armed conflicts in Central America were seen by all the major protagonists as more than simply the result of social and political contradictions, but *as a means to bring about change*. In the 1970s and 1980s, the governments and Armed Forces of Central America viewed war as part of their cold-war 'counter-insurgency' policies. For the armed opposition and their supporters, war was a form of struggle which would eventually bring to power a vanguard to represent the interests of the poor majority (a view strengthened by the Sandinistas' successful overthrow of the Nicaraguan dictator, Anastasio Somoza). It is thus hardly surprising to find that civil-society organisations, especially the popular movements and those who worked alongside them, themselves underwent a huge range of experiences.

It is widely agreed that in cases of acute armed conflict, the civilian population depends on external aid only to a small degree (between 10 and 15 per cent). In Central America, the levels of international assistance were far higher than this, particularly in Nicaragua, and this undoubtedly had a major impact. However, it is questionable to what extent such co-operation directly guaranteed the survival of those most affected. First, every community responds to crisis differently, depending on its composition, its history, and its culture. But since the very poorest communities live in a permanent emergency (especially in relation to food security and health-care), they have a stronger tradition of solidarity than other communities. In order to survive, people rely on each other for meeting material or emotional needs.

In terms of the conflict-related emergency, civilian populations in Central America found themselves in three basic types of situation: communities that lived in areas under guerrilla control, who were either active supporters, or at least were not openly opposed to the guerillas (such as the settlements in the former conflict zones in El Salvador); communities that had direct experience of attacks by either side (for example, some communities in Nicaragua's border areas); and communities that, whatever their own political sympathies, happened to live in disputed areas and therefore suffered almost constant persecution (such as the Communities in Resistance or CPR and others in Guatemala, which fled to the mountains where they survived clandestinely for years).

The Salvadoran communities were highly organised, having developed and consolidated their skills and capacities while they lived in refugee camps in Honduras. Initially, these communities survived thanks to emergency assistance in the form of food aid, basic housing, and medicine. This was channelled through community-based organisations, the churches, and various NGOs set up for this purpose. Gradually, these communities began to produce their own food, and to develop their own health-care and education services. The displaced in Nicaragua were also given emergency assistance

by the churches and certain state-connected NGOs. This constrained their development as communities, and encouraged a high level of dependence on foreign aid (this also happened elsewhere, to varying degrees). The CPR in Guatemala were constantly on the move, and had for many years depended on international aid and the little that they were able to produce for themselves. Although they did manage to produce a little and to develop their own social services, it was not until the peace negotiations began that they could develop openly as communities.

However, large sectors of the population did not fall into any of these three categories. People who had been in the thick of the fighting, and who then lost their social connections as they dispersed throughout the urban areas, had to survive as best they could. As the effects of the SAPs began to be felt, the displaced population contributed to the growth of the informal sector — a sector whose potential of development falls outside any of the published economic data.

In Nicaragua, popular organisations grew in number and strength on an unprecedented scale during the war, mobilising around their own demands and claims. However, these organisations were fairly muted in relation to the state since, as one trade union leader put it, 'we weren't going to attack something we were part of'. This ambivalence reflects very clearly the contradictions in which a revolutionary movement becomes entangled in trying to meet the expecations of the poor — on whose suppport it depends — when it comes to power in such precarious conditions. Nevertheless, it is also true that the levels of social cohesion and organisation were gradually eroded by the economic crisis and the fact that military service was obligatory for so long.

In El Salvador, the popular organisations — especially in the rural areas and in the principal conflict zones — were very 'belligerent'. The civilian population managed to survive under fire, in the later years largely thanks to international support, but in incredibly difficult conditions and in almost total isolation from the rest of the country. As long as access to these areas was so heavily restricted and controlled by the military, the civilian communities also faced huge difficulties in moving around. However, they began gradually to organise not only to address their survival needs but also to protect their communities: it was not uncommon, for instance, to see groups of women trekking to the army barracks to demand the release of

51

community members who had been detained. These people also mobilised in order to get basic services in areas of the country where the state provided virtually nothing; and to demand training for health promoters, education workers, and so on. Initially, this work was supported by Salvadoran NGOs and the churches, but eventually the local population began to take over their management.

In Guatemala, there had been a strong co-operative movement and thriving NGO community since the 1960s, often working with the indigenous indian authorities in the rural areas. With the conflict, almost all forms of popular organisation were dismantled, and the leaders suffered badly. Thus, most humanitarian work had to be carried out clandestinely, especially if it aimed to help those who were most severely affected by political repression and violence. Even so, many NGOs did manage to survive in the conflict zones, albeit in extremely difficult conditions.

In each of the above examples, the civilian population took advantage of any opportunity to improve their own capacities and managed to survive with a minimum of foreign aid, even as they were suffering the worst effects of the war. Undoubtedly, the constant risks and insecurity also created a profound sense of group identity. This in turn gave civilian populations the strength to deal with the situation — and to make demands of their own.

In Central America, 'civil society' was for many years seen simply as existing in contrast to the state, the concept has seen a revival in the post-cold war context. While popular and grassroots organisations invoke it in terms of achieving or expanding citizens' participation in decisions at a political level, the state and MLAs are also interested in such participation from a neo-liberal perspective, seeing this as a means to reduce public services (Pearce, 1994).

It is important to stress, however, that during the worst years of the armed conflict, the term 'civil society' was seldom used, and was generally seen by NGOs and popular organisations as a political construct used to create an apparently homogeneous society out of an economically and socially polarised one. International NGOs instead used criteria which were guided by their own analysis of the extent to which their counterparts clearly represented the poor and excluded, and of the capacity of these counterparts to influence the wider process of social and political change, and to channel assistance to those affected.

Throughout the region, international NGOs supported (and continue to support) a wide range of civil-society actors in their organisation; but they did so with the aim of increasing these actors' capacity to bring about policy changes in favour of the poor majority. During the war, humanitarian aid for civilians in the conflict zones was channelled mainly through intermediary NGOs and church-based organisations. These were seen to have unique access to civilians in these areas, and have their trust. Their analytical capacity and ability to put forward constructive options were also important — especially during the early 1980s when, for reasons already described, few international NGOs had access to the regions of El Salvador and Guatemala where this humanitarian work was being carried out.

At the same time, organisations dedicated to analysing and disseminating information were also supported, in order to allow expression of alternatives to the official versions of events, which were generally either part of the counter-insurgency effort, or which simply concealed what was actually happening, especially in the rural areas where the conflict was most intense.

Support for popular organisations focused on strengthening their organisational capacity (sometimes from their establishment through to their emergence as fully-fledged bodies) and their role in distributing humanitarian aid. Initially, particularly in El Salvador and Guatemala, this was delivered to them through intermediary NGOs. Later, support for popular organisations began to shift towards training and implementing development projects. In Central America, the respective roles of NGOs and popular organisations have been the subject of fierce debate: the former have generally been seen as offering technical assistance, or serving as intermediaries of the main political protagonists. However, local NGOs increasingly claim a role as civil-society actors in their own right, with their own proposals and ideas to put forward.

Institutional relations with local and national actors

Experience in Central America makes it difficult to imagine a community, country, or region in which there are no 'appropriate' counterparts through which international aid agencies can work. Even in the most remote and isolated locations, there are forms of community organisation that can receive supported and/ or act as channels through which to assist others. Where these were relatively weak, external support focused on strengthening their organisational capacity. The churches in Central America were also a vehicle through which to promote local organisational capacity, and to support projects to provide training and community infrastructure. Since there has always been a strong organisational tradition in the region, many international NGOs tried as far as possible to support local capacity-building efforts, and to minimise dependence on financial or technical assistance. In the areas where the conflict was most intense, and which agency staff could therefore not visit, it was often still possible to channel assistance through networks of people from the affected countries, some of whom were based abroad. Essentially, this meant being prepared to accept the risks involved in not being able to monitor these relief efforts directly.

In discussions about the kind of relationship an international NGO had — or would have liked to have — with its counterparts, there were always two major questions: the role of such agencies in 'accompanying' the processes and their local counterparts, especially in high-risk situations of armed conflict; and the concept of 'partners', a term generally used in aid agencies, rather than 'counterparts'.

In general, both counterparts and international aid agencies valued 'accompaniment' as highly as the grant-funding, in some cases more so. In some ways, the mere presence of the international organisations provided some kind of guarantee of safety — in extreme cases, it ensured people's physical survival, especially in El Salvador and Guatemala. For the most part, the agencies who took on this kind of role were like-minded and shared other characteristics; and in El Salvador, this accompaniment was undertaken in a highly co-ordinated way.

As for 'partnership', discussions revolved around the recognition that there are unequal power relations between an international aid agency, which has its own resources and agenda, and local counterparts who have no resources and are in a disadvantaged position vis-à-vis national and international decision-making fora. Some agency workers argued that recognising this inequality was the only basis for a frank and direct relationship with its counterparts; and that one 'partner' having the money should not determine the basis of the relationship. Today, most international NGOs acknowledge this underlying inequality, although many seek to establish more 'horizontal' relationships with their counterparts.

What about planning, evaluation, and impact assessment?

In its formal sense, planning was virtually impossible during most of the war years, especially when the conflicts were at their height. First, the nature of the emergency meant that the situations were highly volatile: one always had to be ready to adapt rapidly to the demands, risks, limitations, and possibilities arising from each situation. Matters were further complicated by the various natural disasters that came on top of the conflict [for example, the 1985 earthquakes in Mexico; the 1986 earthquake in San Salvador; the 1987 hurricane in Nicaragua; as well as many less dramatic cases of floods, droughts, volcanic eruptions, and major industrial accidents — translator's note]. Second, the institutional culture prevailing in many of the international NGOs did not allow any time for proper planning; instead, they either planned in an ad-hoc fashion, or constant changes and domestic restructurings created new demands and new priorities for their regional offices. Finally, the highly polarised political context also affected both the international and local NGOs who assumed that 'flexibility' was synonymous with a lack of planning. In other words, they felt that they had to respond to demands as and when they arose.

As far as evaluation is concerned, few if any international NGOs succeeded in defining a concept and methodology that matched their own institutional expectations and demands. Many counterpart organisations in Central America also resisted the idea of evaluation, both on grounds of security and because of their relative lack of technical capacity. Hence, during the worst of the conflict, international assistance had to be 'evaluated' in unconventional ways, but sometimes without a clear approach and sense of direction.

However, most of the international NGOs underwent an abrupt change as soon as the peace negotiations began to take shape or accords were signed. The peace processes coincided with the end of the cold war, and with new challenges to Northern NGOs in terms both of fund-raising and of new frameworks for official co-operation. In response, the aid agencies began to insist on standards of professionalism as well as planning and evaluation capacities, for which there had been absolutely no preparation during the war. There was a huge gulf between these new requirements — which must be met if NGOs are to survive in the new global political climate — and the reality of trying to develop the necessary skills in the midst of a transition from war to peace. This is a major issue, but one that has yet to be adequately addressed by NGOs in North and South, as well as by other actors involved in international aid.

During the 1980s, particularly when the conflicts were at their height, many NGOs and others in Central America resisted the traditional Northern approach to measuring impact. Some reasons for this emerged from interviews with Central American NGOs, and grassroots and popular organisations:

• In situations of intense armed conflict, and certainly in Central America, impact was judged in terms of people's expectations of structural change. Thus, it was not the impact of projects, programmes, or specific activities that was measured, but rather the relationship between these and the overall 'situation, with a view to bringing about structural changes at the macro level.

• While it is not unusual for international NGOs and national actors to enter some kind of alliance, the question of power (in terms of material resources or access to information) is ever present. Anything perceived as external interference in national affairs is therefore resented. Here, the role of international co-operation has not always been clearly and explicitly defined by both parties. Any such ambiguity is heightened by a concept of evaluation that assumes that one party is going to be analysed and 'sentenced' by the other. In other words, the power that is implicit in the aid relationship becomes explicit in a one-way fashion and not within the framework of mutual co-operation.

• The nature of the work being supported during the acute conflicts throughout the region meant that most efforts were directed towards ensuring survival, with little or no opportunity either to reflect on and 'systematise' this experience, or to consider other kinds of intervention. The dynamic of constantly responding to urgent demands not only limited any existing capacity to measure the impact of what they were doing, but also served to disempower many actors who were thus unable to put all their capacities to best use. While this phenomenon is most dramatically seen in the case of national organisations and actors — who were necessarily part of the process itself — the same dynamics affected most of the international aid agencies.

• The political conflict in Central America was expressed mainly between the warring parties, and far less in the dynamics within the popular and progressive movements themselves. Their identities were linked with their political allegiances, and the various ways in which these were expressed were often very closely tied up with the physical and political survival of these groups and individuals. Thus, attempts to measure the impact of supporting specific projects and groups were often thwarted by the difficulty of grasping the various motivations and political complexities that might be governing their actions.

In spite of these limitations, it was possible to establish certain mechanisms for establishing how projects and programmes were developing. [The term 'seguimiento' or 'follow-up' is used here, as opposed to monitoreo or 'monitoring'. This implies a process of accompaniment, rather than top-down checking — translator's note]. For instance, since it was very dangerous to visit projects in the conflict areas of Guatemala, the representative of an aid agency who visited once a year would share information with other relevant organisations. Thus, some first-hand, albeit not detailed, information about projects was available. But in extreme situations such as these, the clearest indicator of impact is that the population survives at all.

In some cases, for instance in El Salvador, NGOs gradually gained access to the conflict zones, to provide humanitarian aid to the civilian population. This access was the result of systematic lobbying and pressure exerted on the Salvadoran government by national and international agencies, in close co-ordination with the churches and representative organisations. Bit by bit it became possible to visit these areas, although this meant negotiating many military checkpoints — always a security risk, given that the armed forces still regarded anyone who wanted to enter the conflict zones as 'suspicious' (Thompson, 1996; 1997). Since most of the assistance at this stage was for emergency infrastructure such as basic housing, the immediate impact was visible while the technical support was continuing. However, it was only possible to evaluate the social impact years later, once the situation had normalised. By contrast, in Nicaragua it was easier to form technical evaluations of the impact of contra attacks on water supplies, agricultural production, the situation of co-operatives, and other projects based in the war zones.

Involuntary migration and displacement

There were massive levels of both cross-border and internal displacement during the conflicts in Central America, especially in El Salvador, Guatemala, and Nicaragua; and to a lesser extent in the other countries. Thousands of refugees (unofficially estimated to be over 1 million) left their countries of origin as the conflicts intensified. These people either sought asylum in neighbouring countries, or tried to make their way to the USA. Many hundreds were forced from their homes and became internally displaced.

Overall, the international NGOs' position on repatriation was clear: they would respect the refugees' own decisions concerning their return to their countries of origin. However, once they had decided to go back, it was a priority to support them in every possible way. Nevertheless, this support always happened within the framework of the refugees' insistence on some guarantee for their security and dignity. The question of whether the international NGOs would help to prolong the period of exile or encourage the refugees to return was simply answered by reference to what the refugee population and its representatives actually wanted. At the time, few if any NGOs discussed this issue in more depth.

With the benefit of hindsight, perhaps more thought should have been given to what kind of broader capacity-building activities were needed to equip the refugees to deal with the realities to which they would be returning. Yet, given that the vast majority were peasant farmers, the single priority was and continues to be agriculture. Indeed, the refugees were sometimes more experienced and capable than the small-scale farmers in the host countries. For instance, in the Soconusco area of Chiapas, Guatemalan refugees were very much sought after as efficient — and, of course, cheap — farm labourers.

In the case of the Guatemalan refugees in various parts of Mexico, international assistance arguably served to encourage their return. However, many opted to remain in Mexico not only because the overall conditions are better than those they would find in Guatemala (although the assistance they were receiving in Mexico has now been sharply curtailed); but mainly because they have been discouraged by the continuing insecurity in their own country. At the same time, prolonged exile (over ten years in most cases) also has implications for young people's identity, who often prefer to stay where they are. Indeed, some of the Guatemalans in Mexico who were repatriated later returned to Mexico.

Among the various actors which took on responsibility for populations displaced by the conflicts, NGOs played and continue to play a critical part, first in channelling humanitarian aid and then in giving technical advice. However, this has not been an easy process for them. There is a real debate about the role that NGOs should play vis-à-vis the affected population: many popular organisations believe that NGOs should 'serve' them and their interests, while a growing number of NGOs believe that they are civil-society actors in their own right, particularly in terms of their engagement with political processes. Many local NGOs argue that they have the right to define and defend their own positions within civil society, *in support of* popular groups rather than being uncritically *at their service*. This is a region-wide debate at present.

In Nicaragua, NGOs which were very closely linked to the state in the 1980s when the major population displacements took place, helped to organise and orient the internally displaced populations, but had little direct influence among the Nicaraguan refugees, especially those in Costa Rica. In El Salvador the church played the major role in opening up access to the war zones, setting up an ecumencial NGO (Diaconia) which for some years was the main point of reference for humanitarian work in these areas. Later, new NGOs were able to get involved in capacity-building, channelling assistance to the conflict areas, and getting actively involved in specific lobbying, as well as influencing international opinion on the question of refugees and their repatriation. Gradually, the refugee and displaced populations themselves began to deal directly with the aid agencies and to participate in national and international debate. Throughout El Salvador, they formed their own organisations, prioritising their own organisational capacity and assigning the NGOs either a merely technical role, or one of mediation and co-ordination. In Guatemala, the refugees nominated their own representatives to negotiate with the government on how their return should be organised. The NGOs were the main channel for non-government assistance to the refugees in Mexico, together with the Catholic church.

On the international stage, UNHCR was a central player, because of its role as protector and its physical proximity to the refugee population. In El Salvador, under an ad-hoc agreement with the government, UNHCR was able to extend this role to cover the internally displaced population. This was critical in terms of guaranteeing their security and organisational capacity. Unfortunately, it was not possible to do the same in Guatemala, where the UN had no previous presence in the country; as part of the peace process, it was given the task of verifying the human-rights situation. The UNHCR's knowledge of each of the countries in which it was based — as well as its direct communication with the refugees, the intermediary agencies, political actors, and national governments — fundamentally shaped its future role in the region. The UN Missions that have been established in the context of the Peace Accords are different. In their role in the field of human rights, it is precisely the level of trust they can establish which will give them access to the information that should shape their analysis and decision-making.

International NGO support for the refugee and displaced population was offered at various levels:

• Training in productive and other skills, with a view also to enhancing people's capacities on their return home.

• Dissemination of information about events in their respective countries and the host countries, in order to enable them as far as possible to take well-informed decisions. In El Salvador and Guatemala, this role was undertaken largely by the churches and by the refugees' own organisations.

• Lobbying activities, usually in co-ordination with other agencies. These were focused on governments, multilateral agencies, and the UN, with a view to helping to resolve specific problems, facilitating assistance to the civilian populations, or pressing for policies that were in accordance with humanitarian law.

• Participation in regional fora. Here, the CIREFCA experience played a key role in stimulating international co-operation, perhaps a unique experience both in terms of the overall process in Central America, and because of what it ultimately achieved. (CIREFCA was convened by the region's presidents under the auspices of the UN to analyse and seek solutions to the problems of refugee and displaced populations. Representatives from multilateral and bilateral agencies also attended, and national and international NGOs gradually began to participate in and shape the process.)

• Physically accompanying the refugees both in the camps, and sometimes also during the actual return. While such accompaniment was not permanent, this occasional presence had a crucial impact in terms of the trust established with the refugees and their representatives. This provided access to information that was valuable for the work of the international aid agencies, and also helped to reduce the margins for error, which, in highly polarised settings, might have had a high cost either for them or for their counterparts.

The experience of women refugees and internally displaced

Experience in Mexico and Central America sheds some light on ways in which displacement affects women and men differently, although such variations are also profoundly affected by social class, ethnic identity, and the place of refuge, as well as the circumstances and relationships peculiar to each context. That said, we would identify the following common issues:

• Women are, are perceived to be, or may become (even before the experience of displacement) the 'emotional pillar' that guarantees the family's ability to hold together. In Guatemala, for instance, many men in the rural areas and among indian communities were either involved in the war, had been killed, or were 'disappeared'. This meant that the women very suddenly had to take on responsibilities for which they were not prepared. Often, these women spoke no Spanish, and had never set foot outside their own communities. In every one of the interviews conducted in the course of this study (as well as in other testimonies), the top priorities for most women were physical survival and the well-being of their children.

• Women often took on an informal mediation role in handling local and family conflicts. In Siuna on the Atlantic Coast of Nicaragua, for instance, women have tried to mediate in the old conflicts that have arisen again between ex-Sandinistas and ex-*contras*, feuds that are often fuelled by alcohol. One women's organisation has tried to bring together and analyse its experience, and to reflect on the implications of women's unrecognised role in post-war reconstruction.

• In situations of heavy armed conflict, when lives are in real danger, many women not only had to maintain their families alone, but also had to protect their children from the possible risks by 'inventing' stories about where their husbands were. This was certainly an issue for the wives of men who had joined the guerrilla organisations, but also affected those whose husbands had been killed or 'disappeared', who feared that they would be subject to revenge attacks if their situation became common knowledge. As one Salvadoran refugee in Mexico put it, 'we all had to go through a kind of death, to make sure they didn't kill us for real' (from a testimony taken by the Mexico City Support Committee for Refugees).

Human-rights work

Much human-rights work in Central America was focused on education and promoting the recognition of human rights as something far more than the right to life. Although this wider definition was broadly accepted in the region, as the violence became more intense throughout the 1970s, the right to life had become the main focus and driving force for all human rights-related work. As people began to win certain guarantees for the right to life, especially after Esquipulas II, the concept of human-rights work began to expand. Even so, the right to life continues to be one of the most important human-rights claims, especially in Guatemala.

In this setting, human-rights commissions began to emerge throughout the region, often with international NGO support. The commissions later formed a region-wide co-ordination structure, although each commission maintained its autonomous identity. During the 1980s, these commissions and other bodies played a critical role in denouncing human-rights violations, especially in El Salvador and Guatemala. They also created opportunities for publicising information, lobbying, and exerting international pressure, which in turn made it more difficult for abuses to continue to be committed with impunity. Educating people about human rights was often an uphill struggle, especially given the levels of repression and fear prevailing in most of Central America. Interestingly, the Honduran Human Rights Committee (CODEH) made an important contribution in this area. Although Honduras was a key player in the regional conflict — as a base for the Nicaraguan *contra*, and a channel of US support to them — the fact that it did not have an armed conflict in its own territory perhaps meant that, in spite of intense political repression, human-rights education work could address the wider social, economic, and political dimensions. Another important inititative was the training of human-rights promoters. In Guatemala, many of these were trained by Mexican church-based agencies when they were refugees. This enabled them to present human-rights education as central to the life and development of their communities.

Women's rights were rarely regarded as a separate issue during the war years, but were seen instead in terms of the rights of poor people in general. In Nicaragua, however, the revolution served to promote a greater social awareness of women's issues, and also encouraged women to form an organisation of their own (though not without major debates over the question of whether this organisation should be politically autonomous). In El Salvador and Guatemala, it was not until the peace-negotiation processes began that organisations emerged to defend and raise public awareness of women's rights.

The role of international NGOs in mediation and reconciliation

Opportunities for mediation and reconciliation during the armed conflicts in Central America arose at different times and at various levels. On the one hand, the UN's role *par excellence* is that of mediator in peace negotiations. However, other individuals and institutions also played a significant part — though not publicised or widely known — in terms of facilitating 'spaces' or *loci* within which to stimulate dialogue between actors on opposite sides of the conflict. Such spaces for exchange and dialogue were opened up between, for example, business entrepreneurs and workers, between entrepreneurs and members of the armed opposition, between people belonging to political parties and members of popular organisations. This facilitation was generally characterised by an absence of a pre-defined agenda, allowing for a trust-building process to take place, rather than pushing either side to make advance commitments. The fact that these efforts were handled in such a low-profile manner helped in this respect. At the same time, the involvement of certain individuals (often with some institutional backing) inspired mutual trust and conferred a sense of legitimacy.

International NGOs did fund some of these efforts in Nicaragua and El Salvador, although it was not always possible to document their involvement, given that these efforts remained highly discreet. In Guatemala, various agencies helped to introduce the concept of humanitarian aid to those unfamiliar with it, and to link up national NGOs with popular organisations which had sprung up and developed among the refugees and exiles in Mexico, solidarity-based organisations, international NGOs, national actors, and so on.

It is this kind of 'accompaniment' — often not apparent in formal, written information, and sometimes hard to articulate in the context of the war or to translate into the institutional language of the aid agencies — that underpins the trust placed by Central American NGOs and popular organisations in some of the international NGOs. In the end, it is this kind of trust that allows an international agency to understand what is going on within any given context, and so become a reference point for other international actors.

Table 4: Shifting trends in international NGO programmes durnig the armed conflicts in Central America

Period	Main events and processes in the region	Main external events and processes	Main programme focus	Typical counterparts
Up to 1979	Triumph of Sandinista Revolution Rise of popular and revolutionary movements in the region Selective repression against popular leaders and intellectuals; deterioration in the human-rights situation in El Salvador, Guatemala, and Honduras Military governments in most of the region; militarisation of Central American societies	USA withdraws from Somocista dictatorship Mexico gives active support to Central American popular movement International support to Nicaragua following Sandinista triumph	Support for organisational work and strengthening of community and popular organisations Emergency support for victims of repression Analysis and dissemination of information	Trades unions co-ordinating bodies Micro-regional NGOs Church (micro-level) Human-rights organisations linked to the church Co-operatives
	Massive and generalised repression aginst popular organisations, especially in El Salvador and Guatemala; more selectively in Honduras Social organisation and humanitarian assistance undertaken by or for popular organisations and other groups forced underground Massive internal and cross-border displacement Armed conflict affects the entire region, with the exception of Costa Rica Economic crisis and capital flight Coups d'état Changes in the Sandinista government in Nicaragua Intensification of the war in Nicaragua, and the role of Honduras as a *contra* base Outbreak of war at a national level in EL Salvador; fierce attacks against the revolutionary	US government policy under Reagan hardens towards Sandinista government, and the perceived Communist threat in Central America, within a cold-war framework Mexico recognises and 'legitimises' Salvadoran armed opposition, and actively supports Sandinista government International isolation of Guatemala because of human-rights record US government supports Nicaraguan contras	Emergency support for victims of repression Support for productuion and infrastructure in Nicaragua Start-up and ongoing support for human-rights organisations Emergency assistance and support for producition to ensure survival of refugee and displaced populations Support for organisational development and training for popular organisations and co-ordinating bodies Participation in CIREFCA process and support for co-ordination between national and international NGOs Development of analysis and reduction in information work	Ecumenical co-ordintaing bodies NGOs working from exile Local church-based organisations National NGOs Popular organisations (peasant farmers, trades unions) Co-operatives and federations of co-operatives 'Alternative' information agencies Human-rights organisations

Table 4: Shifting trends in international NGO programmes durnig the armed conflicts in Central America *continued*

Period	Main events and processes in the region	Main external events and processes	Main programme focus	Typical counterparts
1985-90	Armed conflicts in El Salvador and Guatemala Esquipulas process acknowledges structural roots of the conflicts Elections and/ or civilian governments in several countries Process of dialogue, with obstacles and interruptions, between governments and armed opposition Human-rights abuses Gradual realisation that no military solution to the regional conflicts would be possible Return of Salvadoran refugees from Honduras Rise of drug trafficking US invasion of Panama FSLN loses Nicaraguan elections	Consolidation of neo-liberal economic model World-wide detente, and political changes in Eastern Europe US government slowly recognises need for negotiated solutions in Central America Increasing US intrervention to halt drug trafficking Global economy restructured into regional trading blocs New right-wing governments in Latin America	Support for returned populations Instituional stregthening Support for regional co-ordinating bodies Training for and development of lobbying strategies Production activities Analysis and information Economic alternatives Conflict resolution Gender-related work	NGOs connected with support structures elsewhere in the region Church groups Trades unions co-ordinating bodies Research centres Women's groups Co-operative movement Human-rights organisations Refugees and displaced persons Popular organisations Regional government and other structures in Atlantic Coast of Nicaragua Urban-beasd groups in Mexico Regional co-ordinating bodies
1990-96	UNO coalition government installed in Nicaragua; demobilisation of the *contra* and reduction of Army commences Peace Accords signed in El Salvador (1992) and Guatemala (1996) Transition and redefinition of roles for civil-society institutiones and actors Civilian governments throughout the region Outbreak of armed conflict in Mexico Worsening poverty for most Central Americans Regrouping of political parties both left and right Rise in common crime and drug trafficking	Bi-partisan US policy tips balance in favour of negotiation International support for peace in the region Consolidation of new economic blocs; economic globalisation Rise in the fight against drugs trafficking Restrictions on migration to the North		Regional co-ordinating bodies National NGOs Micro-regional NGOs Peasant farmer organisations Women's organisations Popular organisations Indian organisations

59

Chapter four: Conflicts and peace in Central America — some reflections

This chapter draws on over 40 interviews and meetings with a wide range of organisations: NGOs, grassroots and popular organisations, women's groups, indigenous people's associations, and with ex-combatants, and individuals. The interviews dealt with the following topics:

- the participation of civil society in the peace negotiations;
- the most important continuing or new conflicts;
- the role of international co-operation during and after the armed conflicts;
- the psycho-social consequences of armed conflict on those directly affected by it.

Civil society in the negotiation processes

'Formally speaking, civil society did not participate in the negotiations. These were between the USA, the contra, and the Sandinista government.' (Nicaraguan NGO spokesperson)

'It wasn't easy to have to see the enemy as simply a political opponent. At the end of the day, our loved ones were still dead, and nothing much had changed.' (Ex-FMLN fighter in El Salvador)

'They haven't seriously taken us into account. We ought to have been at the negotiating table too ... Most of us don't even know what the Peace Accords say. Parts of the document are being translated into our languages, but most of us can't read anyway.' (Mayan indian in Guatemala)

In none of the three countries examined was there any formal participation by civil-society organisations in the peace-negotiation processes. Essentially, the opposing parties became engaged in processes which did not allow for any such direct involvement. This was despite of the fact that the respective negotiations were concerned not only with bringing about a formal cessation of hostilities, but also with addressing the underlying problems that lay at the heart of the conflicts. To some extent, Nicaragua is an exception: here, negotiations focused largely on demobilisation and on reforming the military, in the context of elections which also served to defuse the conflict.

Thus, the peace negotiations in El Salvador, Guatemala, and Nicaragua were not the outcome of any open discussion or consensus involving civil society. While there was a general desire for peace — coupled with the belief that the armed struggle would not succeed in achieving structural change — the negotiation processes came about largely as the result of pressure on both sides. From within, there were the social, economic, and political factors weighing on each party. External pressures included the major changes brought about by the end of the cold war, the need for stability as a precondition for economic globalisation and market-led growth, and the fact that the USA was turning its attention — and its foreign aid — from Central America to other areas of the world.

Interestingly, despite the lack of formal participation, most of those interviewed felt that they had in fact been involved in some way. For example, some had joined in initiatives which had begun in the midst of the conflict, to define and eventually present specific proposals to the negotiating parties — for example, the Civil Society Assembly in Guatemala and the Permanent Committee of National Debate in El Salvador. In other cases, such as that of the Peace Commissions in Nicaragua, efforts were focused more on facilitating and mediating in discussions between the various parties.

More subjectively, however, many Central Americans feel that they made an important contribution not so much in determining the outcomes of the negotiations, but in putting an end to the war and bringing about peace. Civil-society organisations believe that their own desire for peace had a decisive effect in bringing the fighting to a close. Ex-combatants expressed this most clearly in their willingness to lay down arms. However, rather than necessarily seeing this as a deliberate decision to seek reconciliation, many argued that every possibility of finding a solution through war had by then been exhausted, and that there was a certain 'inevitability' about bringing this phase to a close: 'It wasn't that we became neutral, it was simply that the war wasn't resolving anything', said one ex-*contra*.

Women in Central America have tended to see peace as a necessity rather than a choice. In armed conflicts, women usually have to take on the responsibility of sustaining their families and communities, because the men are away fighting or are in other ways affected by the conflict. In the words of one Nicaraguan woman:

There were many widows and women who didn't know whether their husbands were dead or alive. So our major concern was for our children. But yes, we wanted peace.

For women, then, peace is intimately bound up with their own security and that of their families, and with their children's survival. In Guatemala, women who may never before have set foot outside their own communities, and who did not speak Spanish (the official language), found themselves suddenly as heads of household in a socio-economic environment which offers few enough job openings for men, and fewer still for women. Further, the absence of their husbands made these women and their families doubly vulnerable, both to suspicion and to the general insecurity facing women who are 'alone', facing sexual harassment or are social rejection. Some women were protected by their communities, while others went into exile. But some women did come to participate actively in community life — often for the very first time. As one widowed Guatemalan indian put it,

I would never have imagined that I would speak in front of so many people. I scarcely dared even to speak Spanish. But my predicament meant that I had to do it, and now I am glad to talk about my situation and about our rights … though I do sometimes get tired.

The most important conflicts today

'The politicians lack any clear programmes for how to get out of the economic crisis, and the country is becoming politically ungovernable for the same reason.' (Nicaraguan NGO spokesperson)

'The political transition made so many demands on us that we could not systematise our experiences as we would have liked, and this has not helped us to put right our mistakes.' (Member of Salvadoran grassroots organisation)

'We are poor, and that's our main problem. Peace is fine, but we want to see real changes.' (Member of Guatemalan grassroots organisation)

Across the board, poverty is seen as the basic problem, particularly so in rural communities. Even when people tried to use the word 'conflict' to talk about social, political, and economic issues, in fact they were often describing poverty as the greatest 'conflict' or the major 'problem'.

'The main problem is that we're extremely poor. How are we going to live in peace with all this poverty, and while we watch our children dying of hunger?' (Guatemalan woman)

Other issues included the general lack of trust in politicians and political leaders; the lack of unified and effective organisation among the poor; the way in which some communities feel that they have been exploited, especially in relation to 'reconstruction'. In general, there is a strong sense that most people expected the end of the war to bring with it major social and economic changes, both for individuals and the cmomunity. Yet such changes have either not been achieved at all, or are considered to have been very slight. This frustration is seen, more or less openly, as a failure of the leaders to keep their promises.

Higher up in the leadership, there tends to be a greater sense of achievement as people weigh up 'what is possible versus what is feasible'. To a large extent, such attitudes reflect the roles which people played both during the war and in the negotiation and reconstruction processes. The greater the direct high-level involvement, the greater the tendency to 'rationalise' the relationship between what is possible and what is desirable, depending on the circumstances. However, this ability to rationalise also depends on how much people knew about the negotiation and 'reconstruction' process. For instance, some grassroots organisations in Guatemala are unaware both of the terms of the Peace Accords, and of the negotiation and implementation processes. So while they know that these processes will affect them, they feel marginalised from them, and sceptical about any possible benefits: 'Yet another political process that has taken place in the capital city rather than in the rural areas [where most of us live].'

In the context of this sometimes profound frustration, alcoholism has tended to generate or perpetuate conflict. On the Atlantic Coast of Nicaragua, many communities complain that alcohol makes people 'revive' their old resentments, and leads to frequently fatal brawls between old enemies. Others see alcohol as an escape route and a channel for their frustrations: a 'free psycho-analyst', as one Guatemalan put it. What is clear is that the level of crime is rising, often associated with alcoholism and drug-addiction. Given that drug trafficking is now fairly widespread in Central America, particularly in Guatemala, the picture is grim.

In Guatemala, the lack of punishment for crimes committed during the conflict is still seen as a fundamental problem, notwithstanding the peace process. During the war, repression and impunity were seen as profoundly linked with politics, as symptoms of a climate of political violence. The situation becomes more complicated, and vulnerability takes on a different feel, when political repression is overlaid also with common crime (such as kidnapping individuals in order to get the ransom money) and drug trafficking. In a way, the war provided some sectors of the population with a sort of protection, as long as they followed the rules of the game. This does not imply that anyone thinks that the war was a good thing. Rather, it is a question of recognising that for some, the post-war period has been associated with a kind of breakdown or chaos which makes them feel more vulnerable than they did when they somehow 'belonged' to something, or had a form of group identity. On several occasions, for instance, in a Salvadoran community in one of the former war zones, I heard people say that they 'missed' how things were during the war. Then, everyone looked after each other; whereas now, everyone is out for themselves:

'Some of our organisations have no resources to keep themselves going or even to get around. This is very sad. Many people have got tired of the whole thing and have just ended up looking after Number One.'

On the other hand, war and terror have also left mistrust between individuals and within communities. This is especially so where community members were responsible for human-rights violations, or denounced relatives or neighbours, or used terror as a means of exercising authority over others. Formally, the Peace Accords call for a clean-up of the military forces and their spy networks, but in practice these are very hard to eradicate. This is in part because they are so firmly rooted not only in the way people are organised, but also in the minds and mentalities both of the victims and of those accustomed to relying on terror tactics as a means of getting what they want. At the same time, peace (in the limited sense of the cessation of armed hostilities) 'legitimises' any existing forms of power, provided these are not based on physical violence; denouncing these becomes harder with the move from collective to individual defence mechanisms. However, people sometimes feel stronger, more able to express themselves, and to speak out about the past with the emergence of new political spaces. Where this has happened, it has been a collective experience, in which an individual or agency has deliberately acted as a catalyst.

The indigenous indian population tends to feel that quite a lot has been gained in terms of their opportunity to participate. While their poverty may have intensified, and their access to basic services may not have improved, at least the negotiation processes placed firmly on the table the issues of inter-ethnic relations, discrimination, and racism. In contrast, at certain stages of the war, such issues were seen even within progressive and revolutionary sectors as merely 'secondary contradictions'.

The same is true of women, though in this case far more coloured by questions such as social class and levels of participation in the war. Issues of gender-based oppression did not necessarily bring women together during the war, at least not at a nation-wide level. However, the current political opening, along with their own accumulated experience, has opened up spaces in which to debate and discuss women's concerns for the first time, as well as making possible their greater participation in the social and political life of each country.

International co-operation during the conflict

'During the war, there were a lot of foreigners here: co-operants, aid agency people, solidarity workers, and so on. A lot of them came 'for the experience', and when they became disillusioned, they just left.' (Member of Nicaraguan popular organisation)

'Co-operation can have a major influence. The right person in the right place at the right time can make all the difference.' (Salvadoran NGO spokesperson)

On both sides of the political divides, international co-operation played a very active role in Central America, both during the armed conflicts and in the transition period. While US aid was clearly directed towards government counter-insurgency programmes throughout the region, and in support of the counter-revolution (the contras) in Nicaragua, European bilateral and multilateral aid (through what is now the European Union) was generally more impartial and always justified as being in support of negotiated solutions.

International NGOs were similarly marked by the polarised nature of the war, and showed themselves to be for or against the revolutionary processes either as a declared option; or because their humanitarian aid was channelled to populations that were — or were perceived to be — politically and ideologically committed to one side or the other.

The interviews reveal major differences between official and non-government co-operation, particularly in the case of those international NGOs which had a long history of supporting the efforts of popular sectors to achieve social change. One significant difference is in the kind of sums involved. Compared with official aid, NGO funding counted for very little. However, Central Americans who had some experience of international assistance are clear that there were other, equally important, issues of quality. During the war, bilateral and multilateral aid went mostly to governments, with little or no participation by national or international NGOs or civil society organisations. While this is now changing in order to bring in greater non-governmental participation, organisations that have been on the receiving end of international co-operation consistently identify two elements that 'make the difference'. The first is that NGOs are more flexible, both because they are not entirely subject to government policies, and because they often have a background and depth of experience that allow them to focus on processes of social transformation rather than on 'quick impact projects'. The second concerns their capacity to 'accompany' these processes, to develop a different level of communication with their local counterparts, and so strengthen still further their focus on long-term processes.

'International NGO support was vital for us popular organisations, especially when we were suffering brutal repression. We really appreciate the people and organisations who stood by us through thick and thin.' (Member of Guatemalan popular organisation)

However, these positive qualities are today the source of the most frequent criticism directed by local counterparts and others at the international NGOs. They maintain that many of these increasingly resemble the multilateral agencies: starting to adopt the same criteria, leaving social processes to one side, and focusing instead on quick impact projects, especially in the area of economic production. As one Salvadoran NGO spokesperson put it:

'The international aid agencies, particularly the NGOs, 'lived through the process with us' and often identified deeply with it. Suddenly, it was all change. The new emphasis was on technical issues, efficiency, efficacy, and so on — but without recognising and taking into account the more subjective elements.'

This is echoed in the experience of a Nicaraguan NGO leader:

'In Nicaragua, the international aid agencies never assumed their shared responsibility for having fostered paternalism. And yet now these same agencies are expecting us to change our ways of working from one day to the next.' (Nicaguan NGO spokesperson)

In the view of one Guatemalan NGO representative, the wider shift in international aid priorities has been exacerbated by the fact that '[m]any aid agency people seem to be disillusioned with what happened in Nicaragua and El Salvador' with the result that 'we are now paying the price'.

Overall, the UN's role in the regional conflicts is viewed positively, in particular that of UNHCR in terms of the return and reintegration of refugees and displaced persons. Similarly, ONUSAL has a good reputation, with criticism focused largely on its huge expenditure and infrastructure; this was viewed as somewhat extravagant in the context of extreme poverty in El Salvador, and especially in the immediate post-war period. Opinions about UNDP are far more mixed. But the basic concern is that since its mandate means that it must work with national governments, this limits its flexibility and often generates mistrust. In addition, the bureaucracy of the UN and other multilateral agencies 'has placed huge limitations on what they can do'.

Local NGOs and popular organisations in all three countries made similar comments on international NGOs. In particular:

• The importance of *accompaniment* — financial, moral, and often even physical — at times when local counterparts were highly vulnerable. Without exaggeration, there were occasions on which this accompaniment averted, or at least reduced, the loss of life. The presence of international NGOs in the war zones of El Salvador served as a warning to the warring parties not to commit human rights abuses against the civilian population (for to do would have a high political cost in terms of international public opinion). It also helped to 'legitimise' this population, which had hitherto been seen as subversive for having chosen to return to areas under FMLN control. National NGOs value very

63

highly the role played by certain international NGOs in this respect, as well as the level of inter-agency co-ordination these achieved in supporting their own efforts and strategies.

• In El Salvador and Nicaragua, some national NGOs believe that the co-ordination among the international NGOs during the period of armed conflict facilitated progress towards a shared global strategy with them, and also served to encourage national and regional co-ordination efforts among themselves. But one Guatemalan NGO representative pointed out that 'there is a lot of talk about our lack of co-ordination, but from our point of view the lack of co-ordination among the international aid agencies is a real problem. We have to spend a lot of time trying to satisfy the individual needs of each one.'

• In El Salvador, some international NGOs were said to have given unequivocal and effective support to the peace negotiation process. This was done indirectly, by supporting the capacities of their local counterparts to influence the process. In Nicaragua, their support may have dwindled after the Sandinistas' electoral defeat in 1990. However, this was a gradual withdrawal, and slightly different from the rest of the region in that much NGO assistance had been channelled through government or semi-autonomous structures, such as the regional governments in the Atlantic Coast.

• In Guatemala, the role of the international NGOs in supporting the peace negotiation process was less marked. Even so, some assisted the Civil Society Assembly, and others helped their various counterparts to put forward their views on what was happening. The complex shifts in the case of the Guatemalan peace negotiations probably made NGOs think twice before trusting and investing in the outcome. It should be underlined, however, that while these opinions are fairly widespread, they have not been backed with quantitative data (the gathering of which lies beyond the scope of this work).

• Throughout the armed conflict, and especially during the worst phases, there were hardly any international NGOs based in Guatemala. Nevertheless, many continued to fund or help in other ways the few local NGOs and popular organisations that managed to survive. Some Guatemalan NGOs consider that the international NGOs could, and should, have played a more active role in legitimising humanitarian and human rights work through having an in-country presence. However, this argument ignores the fact that many Guatemalan NGOs had themselves to observe a low profile about their work and sources of funding during these years, precisely in order to minimise the risk of a clamp-down.

• Most NGOs speak of having slowly established a level of trust with the international NGOs which enabled them to communicate during the war, and to achieve some impact in the midst of armed conflict in spite of all the limitations. Some distinguish between the international NGOs that sought to build such a level of trust, and those that were operational — a way of working that was perceived as a lack of trust in the implementing capacity of local NGOs.

• Many NGOs hold in very high regard the advocacy work undertaken by some international NGOs throughout the war years, attributing this success to their focus on detailed facts about humanitarian work. Although some feel that the NGOs were not political or radical enough, the general opinion in El Salvador and Nicaragua is that advocacy work was a success. This is especially so of the repatriation and return programmes (an opinion shared by the grassroots and popular organisations), particularly in the wake of the CIREFCA process.

• The importance of individual staff members of the international NGOs, especially during and immediately after the war, was repeatedly stressed. People from local NGOs and popular organisations emphasise that it is not merely the institutions, but also the individuals who work within them, who make it possible to build relationships of trust which determine the quality of support, and so make it possible to have free and open discussions and mutual communication. One Salvadoran NGO worker went so far as to say that the role played by a certain international NGO in facilitating dialogue and discussion was qualitatively more important, and had greater long-term impact, than everything done by UNDP during the same period.

• In Nicaragua, it was frequently underlined that many of the large contingent of foreigners within the international co-operation effort, and even more so in the international solidarity movement, came in order to 'experience' a revolutionary process for themselves. However, once the Sandinistas lost the elections in 1990, and everything became far more difficult, many then left. There is a palpable level of frustration and a sensation of having been abandoned just as things were hardest. This sense of abandonment appears still to rankle, since Nicaraguan NGOs and other organisations are now rather reserved in their welcome towards foreigners.

• Certain organisations are now self-critical of their inability to maintain a clear medium and long-term vision throughout the armed conflict. They explain this as having been a result of the demands and pace imposed by the emergency and by the very need to survive; a dynamic in which international NGOs also became completely engulfed. As a Guatemalan popular organisation put it: 'We need to develop our capacities and our strategic vision. But this needs time — as transition needs time — and we haven't received much in the way of support for this.'

In Guatemala, the ink is still wet on the Peace Accords, and while people do have opinions about the way in which the war ended, and the immediate transition phase, it is as yet only in Nicaragua and El Salvador that enough time has passed for it to be possible to gain an all-round analysis of the role played by international NGOs in this period. That said, many Guatemalan organisations think that the degree of disenchantment with the Nicaraguan and Salvadoran peace and reconstruction processes has had negative repercussions on the willingness of international actors to support the Guatemalan process.

In terms of the immediate post-Accord phase, the following concerns stand out most:

• For the popular organisations and NGOs, the transition to peace meant more than just re-adjusting their working methods and priorities. It entailed also reviewing their entire *raison d'être*, and their role in the process. This was particularly so for those organisations that were born within the armed conflict, and had focused mainly on the emergency. In El Salvador and Nicaragua in particular, the process called for reflection and debate about political autonomy, and their role as political elements within civil society. It also meant addressing many internal conflicts about individual and institutional identity in a new context; a context in which structural transformation was no longer a shared goal around which everyone could rally, but one in which the various sectors were reverting to defending their own individual ground.

• Most of the Nicaraguan and Salvadoran NGOs and popular organisations agreed that representatives of international co-operation — and especially the international NGOs — had

begun to demand and apply the business management criteria of efficiency and efficacy. This was assumed to be in part due to domestic pressures on these agencies but also, as Central Americans perceive it, because their positions had 'hardened' in the wake of the failure to achieve structural change in the region.

• These criteria are not necessarily seen as negative in and of themselves. The problem is that many local actors feel that they are being 'imposed', without the necessary support and time being given to assimilate them, and without the aid agencies concerned having analysed the challenges represented by transition. As one popular leader put it, 'you can't have a strategic vision if you don't even know where you stand right now'. Another said that 'strengthening institutions should be seen not just as improving the administration, but also training human resources. But most co-operation agencies are talking only about administrative efficiency.' A Guatemalan NGO further stressed the importance of knowing how to distinguish between administrative efficiency and helping to promote processes of social change.

• Some Salvadoran popular leaders commented that after the Peace Accords had been signed, even 'friendly' international NGOs 'imposed' on them a strategic planning process which lasted almost two years. They added that although they were not obliged to go along with this, doing so was implicitly a condition for further funding. They added that some NGOs had spent thousands of dollars on the strategic planning process.

• While they saw the need for long-term planning, they felt that the methodology was not useful since it was not based on the realities and practices of the local organisations concerned — it wasn't 'workable'. However, they regret that the most serious consequence was that getting involved in these agency-dictated processes meant that they could not attend to their own grassroots membership, and began to focus almost exclusively on brokering projects. They regard this as a 'decapitalisation process in terms of our role and experience as social organisations'.

• As part of this dynamic, popular organisations were also asked about their need for technical personnel who could take up the new challenges being posed by the international aid agencies. However, such personnel could not always accommodate the dynamics of the social movement within their planning frameworks. Such organisations have come to the conclusion that what they need are 'politically committed technical personnel, and technically competent political leaders': the two are inseparable and mutually reinforcing.

• The leaders of some popular organisations still reject anything that smacks of being 'technical', because they associate this with bureaucracy or with losing touch with the grassroots. However, these attitudes are changing, and there is a growing recognition of the need to be skilled in a number of areas, particularly among the local-level leadership.

• There is a general awareness in the region that the war also set up patterns of dependency and paternalism, especially where aid programmes were in operation. However, local organisations complain that the shared responsibility for these negative effects has not been accepted by the international agencies. Further, the aid agencies imagine that such dependence can be rapidly turned around — something that is simply not realistic in situations in which there has been a long history of welfarism.

• Some local organisations, NGOs in particular, flagged up the role that certain international NGOs played during the armed conflicts, in terms of providing information and analysis for key players in the North who otherwise would not have had this access. This was especially true of El Salvador and Guatemala, and was closely linked with the lobbying work mentioned above.

As regards the perception of international co-operation and the involvement of international relief and development agencies today, interviewees stressed the following points:

• Many of the international aid agency workers are new. They did not live through the war years, and do not have a detailed knowledge of the context. This has made working with them far harder, since it is like having to start all over again — which takes up a lot of time. While staff changes are normal, many local observers consider that a good prior knowledge of the working environment is indispensable.

• The level of personal disenchantment with what has happened in the region is an issue not only with Central Americans, but also among aid agency workers. This has had negative effects not only on the level of support offered, but also in terms of the amount of time and trouble that these people are prepared to spend on getting

to understand what is going on. Essentially, either their minds are already made up, or they reject the local leadership out of hand.

• Every popular and grassroots organisation that was interviewed in the course of this study regarded the reduction or cessation of support for organisational work, and the priority given to production, as a major problem. As one Nicaraguan leader put it: 'If we don't have any organisational structure, then we might just as well go it alone. We don't need to work on projects together — what we do need is to unite in order to seek alternatives'. For the social organisations, support for their organisational capacity means the chance to define their own priorities, and to revive the popular movement.

• For local NGOs, these trends translate into a reduced capacity to 'accompany the process'. One Nicaraguan NGO commented that the international NGOs that are supporting them will now allow only 8 per cent of the budget to be spent on administration. This has limited their ability to monitor projects on the Atlantic Coast, since the transport and daily costs both for their own personnel and for the local communities would absorb almost the entire administrative budget. However, there have been limitations on both sides: international agencies have in some cases not taken full responsibility for the commitments they have taken on, and local organisations have not made their needs explicit.

• The lack of 'accompaniment' is most acutely felt within the social movement. During the war, many social organisations believed in the possibility of a major change, and focused their efforts on achieving this. Today, not only have their political reference points disappeared or changed, but they only have a very limited role with respect to formal democracy. It was revealing to hear a Salvadoran trade union leader say that, paradoxically, peace had 'neutralised' their struggle, since the formal structures could not guarantee their rights, while any form of demonstration or pressure on their part was interpreted as 'provocation'. Faced with this, the little support that such organisations now receive for their work limits their chance to consolidate and establish broad-based consensus.

• Along with the new emphasis on administrative efficiency and on measurable impact, many local organisations feel that the international aid agencies have become far more project-focused and short-termist. One

Guatemalan NGO spokesperson put this particularly forcefully: 'We need a qualitative change in how we see international co-operation. If they [the aid agencies] want to talk about being "partners", they have to get involved in the whole process, they have to be flexible in order to make any kind of progress, accepting that there will be partial failures along the way, but still maintaining a long-term vision. To support processes as opposed to a few projects here and there means making at the very least a medium-term commitment.'

• A key element in the view of local actors, which is often under-estimated by the international aid agencies, is the exchange of experience both within and among the countries of the region. There were very few opportunities for this during the war, both because of logistical difficulties, but also because people were very cautious about sharing information about their work for security reasons. With the advent of peace came the chance to work together. However, it seems that support for such initiatives was falling, since such exchanges can seldom demonstrate a short-term or measurable impact.

• Many community-based organisations know very little about the whole aid industry, and even the beneficiaries are unaware of where the money comes from, or how much is earmarked for them. This sometimes generates a certain distrust, but also seriously limits the communities' scope to participate in and monitor the very processes of which they are meant to be a part.

Finally, across the board, it was emphasised that international aid agencies should see development as a set of inter-linked processes including people's survival needs (especially in a war context), but also their dignity as human beings, their capacities and opportunities to have access to resources, as well as to participate in social and political processes.

For many Central American organisations, peace has brought with it a reduction in the amount of international support for their work. They find this very contradictory, and have reached the conclusion that at least some of the aid agencies were simply attracted by the spectacular nature of the war. A worker with one NGO on the Atlantic Coast of Nicaragua put it thus: 'It seems as if we need another armed conflict if we want to attract any international attention, or get any aid'.

There are various views on the shift towards operational projects, and the new tendency of international aid agencies to go direct to local communities, by-passing popular organisations or NGOs. In general, both NGOs and community-based organisations are critical of these trends, arguing that operational projects set up social and organisational dynamics that create something of a vacuum and also interfere with the community's own structures. At the same time, it is appreciated that if (but only if) an outside agency is well trusted, it can sometimes act as a facilitator in local conflict management. Certainly in Guatemala, this new dynamic has created real conflict:

'From the people's point of view, the foreigners arrive with lots of dollars, and we simply can't compete since all we offer is accompaniment … so we lose our legitimacy with our own people.' (Guatemalan NGO representative)

Finally, some people remain sceptical about the involvement of the aid agencies and other international organisations in the processes of reconciliation and conflict-resolution. They feel that some of them became involved without taking into account the real conditions and need for structural change. They also felt that this form of intervention has encouraged some local organisations to see reconciliation and conflict-resolution as a source of funds rather than as a vital part of social transformation. To avoid this risk, it is crucial that any such efforts have the right focus and are also based upon real trust.

The psycho-social consequences of armed conflict

'Let them sign the Accords by all means, but all I'm interested in is making sure that the killers are punished.' (Member of the public in Guatemala)

'I've not felt comfortable as a civilian. I'm always seen as an odd-ball — I felt better before, and I also belonged to a group then.' (Ex-combatant in El Salvador)

'I feel strange, as if I really don't know who I am any more. I used to be a fighter and now no-one will even give me a job. I used to feel that I was respected by others. I'll get over it somehow — there are lots of us in the same boat, and we'll just have to see how we deal with it.' (Ex-combatant in Nicaragua)

Many years ago, Martin Baro, one of the Jesuits who was assassinated by the Salvadoran military, commented that we perhaps must assume that the entire generation who were protagonists and victims of the armed conflicts in Central America have been emotionally damaged. He added that while it might be possible to repair some of this damage at a social and collective level, we must face up to the possibility that the kind of repair that will allow us to build 'healthy' societies would be the task of future generations, since our own had suffered so profoundly. Time is proving him right.

In Central America as elsewhere, the consequences of armed conflict include a psycho-social dimension that is still hard to define or predict, though there is certainly today a level of generalised aggressiveness and related behaviour that has itself created major problems at the local and national level. For many people, the consequences are largely negative. However, it is also true that individuals and groups have found constructive ways in which to channel their grief, their anger, and other feelings arising from the loss of their loved ones, their identity, their hopes. The process of preparing this paper highlighted four distinct types of trauma or emotional conflicts that had been caused by the war, and differences in the ways in which people were trying to overcome these. These differences depended largely on the person's own social background, and the role they had played during the conflict itself.

In Central America, and especially in El Salvador and Guatemala, the military campaigns were not only directed against the rebel movements, but also against the civilians who were considered their support base. In Nicaragua, while the National Resistance did not focus its main attacks on civilians, it did target the social-service and organisational infrastructure. For example, during the years when the *contras* waged war on the Sandinista government, some 300,000 Nicaraguan citizens were left without any access to health services due to the number of clinics that were destroyed by the *contra*. In El Salvador, and even more so in Guatemala, civilians became the main target of military operations in which murders, disappearances, torture, and threats were the 'daily bread' of thousands of ordinary people, who were thus forced to live with fear, and to develop the defence mechanisms that would enable them to survive.

Asking the survivors how they felt at the point when things became most difficult (for example, when one of their family was disappeared), they usually mentioned various somatic symptoms such as fatigue, giddiness, and nausea. Guatemalans talk about *susto* (fright) in similar terms, and consider this to be an illness. Among the elderly in particular, the feeling of vulnerability is often heightened by their being dependent and unable to do anything about the situation; though in some cases, older people are highly respected authorities in the community, and serve as a kind of 'guide' or support in times of conflict.

When terror actually becomes a state policy, the collective social wounds transcend individual suffering. In societies which place a high cultural value on interaction at the community level, even individual trauma is assimilated as something social rather than personal. For the Mayan peoples of Guatemala, the obliteration of their communities did not just mean thousands of deaths, but also the violation and destruction of their environment, their crops, of 'our soul and our identity', in the words of a member of the widows' organisation CONAVIGUA. Even for those who survived, or who did not live in the areas most affected by the fighting,

'Suffering is normal for us ... but there were many who suffered more than we, but they are still part of us ... as indians, and although they didn't kill us, we witnessed how they killed our brothers, and that's just as important to us.' (Indian community leader).

Many people consider that suffering is 'normal' because it is part of their social reality. Suffering relates mainly to discrimination, to poverty, and to the death or sickness of malnourished children. But when an entire way of life is destroyed, this suffering is intensified by the confusion and chaos caused by the fact that society has no means of managing the crisis coherently, nor of offering any way out of the situation. In Guatemala, the terror was lived and acknowledged, but never mentioned by name — even to talk about community organisation or development projects could be construed as 'subversive'. This silence was part of what allowed the atrocities to go on with impunity, and it made it impossible for people even to begin to process psycho-social trauma at any level.

In Guatemala, the question of punishing those who committed human-rights violations is still the subject of debate, and the likelihood is that it will never happen. While there are widespread calls for the guilty to be called to account, for many rural communities the very minimum is that what happened to them should be publicly acknowledged, in proper recognition of their dead and disappeared. Hence the various efforts to make 'symbolic reparation', such as putting up plaques and building local monuments to commemorate those who lost their lives, have assumed real importance in reconstructing the collective memory and reweaving the social fabric. These symbols allow people to begin to process their grief; and as they begin to express their feelings, so they can start to find outlets for their individual and collective concerns. These efforts have mainly been encouraged by the Catholic church, but also by NGOs and other groups who are keen to reconstruct a shared memory. Creating a space that can stimulate public recognition of what took place (vital in contexts where high levels of repression have always been denied), and being able to embrace the difficult emotions this will release, is a huge responsibility. What is needed is not just a catharsis, but also a capacity to accompany those who have suffered and help them to process and channel their feelings in a constructive way.

Children, especially the ones who actually witnessed the killings or saw family members tortured, are themselves tortured by dreams and flash-backs. Their parents say that they are generally withdrawn and frightened of loud noises. Women seem to suffer more than men from depression. One Guatemalan psychologist maintains that

'about 20 per cent of Guatemalan women show signs of depression, which is owing to the fact that they are involved in a constant struggle for survival, and are also having to play a great many roles. During the war, or in the face of terror tactics, women often succumb to being victims of abuse either because of their family situation, or their religious upbringing. They feel the moral burden as well as the fears, and the feelings of guilt.'

There have been few initiatives focusing on the mental health needs of women or children throughout the region, although an increasing number of women's organisations are now paying attention to this in their programmes. At the community level, people are developing their own strategies, which are generally based on co-operation and mutual solidarity. During the armed conflict, many such communities 'took on' the widows and even more so the orphans, preferring to look after them themselves than to hand them to the government authorities or other institutions.

Among the ex-combatants, there has been real difficulty in re-integrating and finding a new role for themselves. The situation is complicated by the fact that they experience social rejection (whether real or as a result of political manipulation), being seen as a potential risk or as delinquents. Individuals who only a short time ago were heroes now find themselves cast as killers; on top of their own loss of identity they suffer anguish and severe depression, and may begin to engage in self-destructive behaviour. Yet it is of strategic importance to analyse and support this sector in the post-war period. First, because the reintegration of ex-combatants is vital in achieving and maintaining peace; and second, because reintegration requires a society to come to terms with its past and its present, and to recognise the need to build a different future — one that is based on respect for diversity, and on a recognition of all the political actors. In both El Salvador and Nicaragua, the ex-combatants are one of the most important groups to have shown their displeasure with the failure to comply with promises and agreements made concerning their social re-insertion. It would hardly be surprising, then, to find that much of the rise in common crime is connected with ex-combatants who were brought up and trained as fighters, and have not found any viable alternatives to this way of life in peacetime.

Of course, many people did develop mechanisms to protect themselves and survive throughout the war, as well as to channel their grief and anguish. But aggression can also be seen as a response to the problems that people now face in meeting even their basic needs. Thus, in addition to any strategies that they or others are able to come up with in the area of mental health, local communities urgently need to have positive signals that things are really changing for the better in terms of their day-to-day lives.

For almost everyone who was involved in the armed conflicts, then, the situation has become more, not less, complicated with the advent of peace. During the war, people had clear roles to play, and a deeply rooted sense of their personal and group identity. Peace-time has meant for them the need to confront all the uncertainties of adapting to a new way of life.

Appendix 1: Summary of the 1992 Peace Accords in El Salvador

The Peace Accords consist of nine chapters, the principal contents of which are summarised below.

Chapter 1: The Armed Forces

This concerns aspects relating to the Principles of Doctrine of the Armed Forces, in accordance with the Constitution and within the framework of principles of a state of law. It includes the establishment of an education system for the Armed Forces, their professionalisation, the purging of corrupt elements, a reduction in their size, the lifting of impunity (referring this matter to the Truth Commission), the creation of a National Civil Police Force, and the abolition of some of the institutions concerned with public security. It also refers to the abolition of existing military intelligence bodies, and the subordination of any future such bodies, as well as the Ministry of Defence, to the civil authorities, to the overhaul of the Infantry and the Immediate Reaction Batallions, the outlawing of paramilitary organs (and regulations governing the reservists as well as any private security services), an end to conscription, and preventive measures to encourage the Armed Forces to comply fully with these provisions, including the relocation and demobilisation of those who belonged to military structures that were due to be suspended or dissolved.

Chapter 2: National civil police force

This refers to the creation of a National Civil Police Force, and addresses issues such as doctrine, functional and territorial structures, personnel qualifications, and its internal management. It also covers the establishment of a Public Security Academy, as well as the judicial regime covering both bodies, and the transitional arrangements.

Chapter 3: Judicial system

This concerns the integration of the National Council and Judiciary, and the establishment and organisation of a National Procurator for the Defence of Human Rights.

Chapter 4: Electoral system

This refers to plans to reform the electoral system.

Chapter 5: Economic and social issues

This argues that sustainable social and economic development in El Salvador is one of the pre-requisites for re-uniting the population. It covers issues such as Agrarian Reform, guaranteeing the transfer of land in accordance with the Constitution and the Agrarian Reform, and an Agrarian Code to fill the gaps and address the various contradictions within existing legislation. This Chapter also addresses the issue of regularising land property rights within the former conflict zones, attending to the demand for agricultural credit, and credit for micro- and small enterprises, and taking steps to alleviate the social cost of Economic Structural Adjustment. The Accord makes general observations on mechanisms for international assistance.

The Chapter introduces plans to establish a Forum for Economic and Social Concertation '… with the equal participation of government, labour, and private enterprise, in order to achieve broad-based agreements on how to foster economic and social development in El Salvador, that would benefit all citizens …'. The Accord also refers to the Salvadoran government's National Reconstruction Plan, which stressed the integrated development of those areas of the country that had been most affected by the war, to be assisted by UNDP.

Chapter 6: Political participation by the FMLN

This refers to guarantees for the civil and political rights of former FMLN combatants; the freeing of political prisoners; guarantees and security for returning exiles, casualties, and others; the granting of mass media licences to the FMLN; the participation of the FMLN and its legalisation as a political party; and the right to spaces within which it could conduct its activities in a normal way. It address the FMLN's participation in the Peace Commission (COPAZ), and various security measures for the FMLN leadership, to be verified by ONUSAL.

Chapter 7: Cessation of armed hostilities

The formal cessation of armed hostilities dates from 1 February 1992, and comprises four elements: cease-fire, separation of forces, the incorporation of the FMLN into civilian life, and the UN verification programme. The Accord contains six annexes outlining how to put its provisions into practice.

Chapter 8: UN verification

Through ONUSAL, and through a specific mandate from the UN Secretary General, the UN would verify compliance with the Peace Accords '... with the co-operation of both Parties and of the competent authorities'.

Chapter 9: Implementation schedule

This defines the schedule and mechanisms for making progress towards compliance with the Peace Accords.

Annexes and additions to the Peace Accords

Finally, the signed Accords contain three Annexes:

- the Bases for Formulating a Law for Authorising, Registering, and Controlling Groups or Organs to Protect the Security of the State, Businesses, Individuals, and Private Security Personnel;

- the Outline of a Law Governing the National Civil Police Force;

- the Outline of a Law on the National Academy of Public Security.

A series of Complementary Accords dealt with outstanding matters which either could not have been foreseen during the principal negotiations, or which needed to be altered in the light of experience. (*Execution of the Peace Accords in El Salvador. Re-scheduling, Complementary Accords, and Other Important Documents, United Nations, 1997*).

Appendix 2: Summary of the main Peace Accords in Guatemala

The Accord on the Identity and Rights of the Indigenous Peoples

This Accord, signed in March 1995, contains the following four chapters.

Chapter 1: The identity of the indian peoples

This chapter deals with relevant constitutional reforms.

Chapter 2: The fight against discrimination

This section defines ethnic discrimination and sexual harassment as crimes, and establishes the government's responsibility for setting up a defence council for indigenous indian women. The Accord further determines that discriminatory laws would be derogated, that information on the rights of indigenous indian peoples would be disseminated, and that the approval and fulfilment of Agreement 169 on Indigenous and Tribal Peoples would be guaranteed.

Chapter 3: Cultural rights

Cultural rights would be furthered by, for example, giving official recognition to indigenous languages within the Constitution, and undertaking educational reform that would respect cultural diversity, while also guaranteeing indigenous indians access to all educational levels. Respect for indigenous spiritual values and practices would be assured, and the government would undertake to adopt anti-discriminatory measures and to make the necessary judicial and bureaucratic changes in order to allow the indigenous indian peoples full access to the means of communication, and to scientific, artistic, and educational information.

Chapter 4: Civil, political, social, and economic rights

These rights would be promoted through government-supported reforms of the Municipal Code in order to allow the indian communities to determine their own priorities and also shape the relevant decision-making processes. The new Code would also address issues relating to the community's own authorities and respect for customary law, provided that these were compatible with the national judicial system. The government would propose legal dispensations to set up mechanisms for defining the scope of the indian authorities' jurisdiction; and also consider ways in which to commit public resources to community development. This chapter of the Accord also set out undertakings to promote the necessary legal and institutional reforms to establish appropriate consultation mechanisms with the indigenous indian populations, and guarantee them access to public positions.

The Accord on Socio-Economic Aspects and the Agrarian Situation

This Accord was signed with the government of Alvaro Arzú on 6 May 1996 and comprised the following four chapters.

Chapter 1: Democratisation and participatory development

This chapter deals with the government's commitment to enact measures designed to guarantee popular participation in public-sector management, both through various mechanisms at community, municipal, departmental, and regional level; and through the Urban and Rural Development Councils, which would in turn serve to promote the Local Development Councils. The government also undertook to restructure its development plans and reform public bodies in such a way that these would ensure special attention to the socio-economic situation of women, particularly in relation to health, housing, work, and skills training.

Chapter 2: Social development

This chapter includes topics such as the government's commitment to restructure the national budget in favour of social spending and public administration, and to guarantee that its management would be efficient, efficient, and accountable. Spending on health and education were to be stepped up by 50 per cent of 1995 levels by the year 2000. Similarly, infant mortality was to be reduced by one half, while health services were to be decentralised and directed towards the poorest. The social security system would be reformed, and 1.7 per cent of the tax revenue would be invested in housing. The government further committed itself to professional training programmes for at least 200,000 workers, while setting a target of 6 per cent annual growth in GDP.

Chapter 3: Agrarian situation and rural development

This part of the Accord focuses mainly on mechanisms through which to implement the government's undertaking to promote an integrated development strategy that would address issues such as land use and tenure, natural resources, credit, legal and technical assistance, and guarantees of sustainability. The chapter's nine sections include participation, access to land and productive resources, the structure of support, the productive organisation of the rural population, the legal framework and juridical security, an official land and property register, workers' protection, and protection of the environment and natural resources.

Chapter 4: Modernisation of public administration and fiscal policy

In this section, the government proposes to raise tax revenue by the equivalent of 50 per cent of the 1995 GDP levels by the year 2000. It also commits itself to strengthening the administration and recovery of taxes, and to reform the tax code in order to make the fiscal system more efficient and accountable, as well as punishing tax evasion and fraud.

The Accord on Strengthening Civil Power and the Role of the Army within a Democratic Society

This Accord was signed on 19 September 1996, and signalled the end of the negotiations on the substantive issues. The provisions of its eight chapters were as follows:

Chapter 1: The state and the form of government; the agrarian situation and rural development

This part of the Accord underlines the need to improve and strengthen the state apparatus in order to further the democratisation process and support civil power.

Chapter 2: The legislature

This chapter proposes that Congress set up a multi-party body to work alongside the legislative commissions charged with addressing the issues arising from the Peace Accords, strengthening and modernising the Congress itself, on the basis of a clear agenda. This body was to be formed no later than three months after the final Accords were signed, and its recommendations brought before the full Congress within one year at the latest.

Chapter 3: The system of justice

In this chapter, the government agrees to reform and modernise the system of justice. It also proposes reforms in the Political Constitution with regard to the legal profession, public service, penal defence, and the penal code. It suggests that the judicial system in general, and the Ministry of Public Affairs in particular, would be better resourced with a view to establishing a Public Penal Defence Service by 1998. With assistance from MINUGUA, the President of Guatemala would also set up a commission made up of public and private professionals to prepare a report and recommendations on the justice system, with special emphasis on modernisation, access to justice, efficiency, professional excellence, and the role of non-government actors.

Chapter 4: The executive

In this chapter, the parties agree on setting up an Advisory Council on Security made up of distinguished personalities and representatives of Guatemalan society, to be nominated by the President. The government agrees to restructure the police forces and to establish a single National Civil Police Force to be charged with public order and internal security, and to be fully operational by the end of 1999 under the auspices of the Home Office. To this end, the government agrees to adopt and to put forward to the Congress further measures relating to constitutional and legal reforms, the organisation of the police force, and the establishment of a recognised professional career through the Police Academy.

The government also commits itself to presenting to Congress a law to regulate private security firms, and to limit the right to hold arms, also under the aegis of the Home Office. The role of the Army would be restricted to defending national sovereignty and the integrity of national territory. No civilian would be tried by a military tribunal. The Accord also establishes that the Minister of Defence could be a civilian or a military officer, and that a new military doctrine is to be developed in accordance with the Political Constitution, human rights, and the spirit of the Peace Accords. There would be reforms in the system of military education, while the size of and resources available to the Army would be 'in accordance with what it needed in order to comply with its role in defending national sovereignty and territorial integrity, and with the country's economic possibilities'. With regard to military and social service, the government agrees to push for a Civil Service law which is currently being developed by a joint team.

The Accord also accepts that the Army might fulfil certain public security functions in exceptional cases, but only as a temporary measure and at the President's discretion. Similarly, the President would establish a body to replace the Presidential High Command that would protect his own security and that of the Vice-President and their respective families.

As far as the state intelligence services are concerned, the Accord proposes the setting up of a Department of Civil Intelligence and Analysis under the aegis of the Home Office; its role would be to gather information in order to combat both organised and common crime. In addition, a civilian-based Secretariat for Strategic Analysis would be set up, with links to the Intelligence Department and the Intelligence Section of the Army's High Command, with the purpose of providing advice and information to the President. The government would aim to prevent the existence of other intelligence groups or networks, and would formulate laws to that effect. The Accord also provides for the transfer of any existing files to the Home Office.

With regard to the right of ordinary Guatemalan citizens to seek public office, the government commits itself to modernising the public administration, to encouraging training and greater professionalism among public servants, and to ensuring that corruption was punishable by law.

Chapter 5: Social participation

Social participation would be addressed via the government's commitment to decentralise public administration by strengthening municipal government and the running of the Development Councils, setting up Local Development Councils, and by creating the conditions for the development of '... local organisations that could represent the people, supporting their participation through education and information about human rights, and reviving the political culture and the capacity to resolve conflicts in a peaceful manner'.

Chapter 6: Women's participation in strengthening civil power

Women's participation would be achieved through the government's commitment to promote campaigns to disseminate information as well as educational programmes to raise public awareness of women's rights, support women's organisations, and ensure that women were represented in all power and decision-making structures. Both parties urge women's organisations to join forces in putting the Accords into practice, especially in those aspects that particularly affect women.

Chapter 7: Operational aspects concerning the cessation of armed conflict

This chapter addresses the demobilisation and disarmament of the Voluntary Civil Defence Committees (known as Civil Defence Patrols), to be completed within 30 days of the derogation of the Decree governing these. Further, these Committees would not be able to reorganise in order to re-establish their relationship with the Army. The Accord also covers the disbanding of the Ambulatory Military Police within one year of signing the final agreements.

The redeployment of Army troops would be completed during 1997: there would be a one-third reduction in the number of men under arms, and the budget would be re-oriented so as to permit a 33 per cent reduction in spending by 1999 in relation to 1995 GDP figures. Military training courses would be transformed in order to reflect the new military education system, and would thus abandon any content relating to the doctrine and practice of counter-insurgency. The government would develop programmes to enable demobilised soldiers to re-integrate into society once the Accord for Firm and Lasting Peace had been signed.

Chapter 8: Final dispositions

The final dispositions concern the request that the UN verify compliance with the Accords, which would come into effect as soon as the final agreement was signed; they also include the commitment to disseminate the terms of the Accord as widely as possible.

Notes

Select Bibliography

1   Oxfam GB was known as Oxfam United Kingdom & Ireland during the period in question, but is abbreviated to Oxfam throughout this paper.

2   In Central America, the word 'counterpart' is preferred to 'partner', for reasons described in Chapter 3. For further discussion on this issue, see Eade and Williams, pp. 127-8.

3   'Popular organisation' is a term commonly used in Latin America to describe organisations which are formed by, and represent, people who are in some way marginalised from social, economic, and political power. Examples of such organisations are women's groups, unions, or associations of small farmers. They differ from community-based organisations in that they tend to have a wider constituency (often nationwide), and seek to influence public policy in favour of their membership. For further discussion, see Eade and Williams, pp. 336-53.

4   Wallenstein and Axell, 1993

5   ibid.

6   Ives, 1987

7   Bishop Gerardi was brutally assassinated in 1998 days after his report on human-rights violations in Guatemala, entitled 'Never Again', had been published (translator's note).

This paper has drawn on a great many internal and published documents of the Frente Sandinista de Liberación Nacional (FSLN) in Nicaragua, the Frente Farabundo Martí de Liberación Nacional (FMLN) in El Salvador, and the Unidad Revolucionaria Nacional de Guatemala (URNG) in Guatemala; and on government documents. Since most of these not readily available and are published only in Spanish, they are not listed here. Likewise, the occasional publications of the Asamblea de la Sociedad Civil (ASC) in Guatemala and of the Comite Permanente del Debate Nacional (CPDN) in El Salvador are not included. The respective Peace Accords and principle related documents are available in English from the UN.

Information has also been taken from various internal Oxfam documents over the period 1979-96, including Annual Reports and Strategic Plans produced by the Regional Office for Mexico and Central America, and a survey of conflict-related work over the period by Oxfam's Emergencies Department. Since these are not public documents, bibliographic details have not been included [Translator's note].

Agerbak, Linda (1991) 'Breaking the cycle of violence: doing development in situations of conflict', *Development in Practice* Vol. 1 No. 3. Reprinted in Eade (ed.) 1996.

Buell, Rebecca et al. (1996) *Oxfam's work in conflict situations*, unpublished mimeo, Oxford: Oxfam.

Choucri, Nazli (1983) 'Population and Conflict: New Dimensions of Population Dynamics', New York: UNFPA.

Centro de Investigaciones para el Desarrollo de Centroamerica (1996) *Guatemala: Situación Actual y Perspectivas – una aproximación para el debate*, Guatemala City: CIDECA.

Comite Co-ordinador de Asociaciones Agricolas, Comerciales, Industriales y Financieras (1994) *Guatemala: Reflexiones del pasado, consideraciónes del presente y recomendaciónes para el futuro*, Guatemala City: CACIF.

Dye, David, Judy Butler, Deen............ng......
and Jack Spence, with George Vickers (1995)
*Contesting Everything, Winning Nothing: The search
for consensus in Nicaragua 1990-1995*, Cambridge,
Mass.: Hemisphere Initiatives.

Eade, Deborah (ed.) (1996) *Development in States
of War*, Oxford: Oxfam.

Eade, Deborah and Suzanne Williams (1995)
The Oxfam Handbook of Development and Relief,
Oxford: Oxfam.

El Bushra, Judy and Eugenia Piza-Lopez (1993)
Development in Conflict: the gender dimension,
Oxford: Oxfam.

Frente Farabundo Martí de Liberación Nacional
(1996) *Los Acuerdos de Paz en El Salvador: Proceso
de Transición 1992-1996*, San Salvador: FMLN
Publications.

Fundación Augusto Cesar Sandino (1995)
*Experiencia de la FACS en el proceso de concertación
y reconciliación en Nicaragua*, Managua: FACS.

Galtung, Johan (1995) 'Transformación de
Conflictos — una visión integral', paper delivered
at the Centro de Estudios Internacionales (CEI) in
Managua.

Inforpress (1995) *Guatemala 1986-1994: compendio
del proceso de paz*, Guatemala: Inforpress
Centroamericana.

Kellma, Alexander (1995) 'Cultura de Paz',
paper delivered at the Primer Congreso
Latinoamericano de Relaciones Internacionales
e Investigaciones para la Paz [no further details
provided – translator].

........, ... (1995) *Sobrevivimos la Guerra*, San
Salvador: Adelina Editores.

Lederach, Paul (1994) *Building Peace: Sustainable
Reconciliation in Divided Societies*, Tokyo: UN
University.

Oberschall, Anthony (n.d.), *Las Teorias sobre el
Conflicto Social*, Nashville, TN: Vanderbilt
University'.

Ortega, Zoilamérica (1994), *Los desmovilizados
nicaraguenses en la construcción de la paz*,
Managua: CEI.

Pearce, Jenny (1996) 'Civil Society in Latin
America' (in draft), Department of Peace
Studies, University of Bradford, UK.

Spence, Jack and George Vickers (1994) *Una
Revoluci and George Vickers (1994) Latin America'
(in draft), Department of Peace Studies, Univer*,
Cambridge, Mass.: Hemisphere Initiatives.

Thompson, Martha (1996 and 1997)
'Empowerment and survival: humanitarian
work in civil conflict', *Development in Practice* Vol.
6 No. 4 (part I) and Vol 7. No 1 (part II).

Voutira, Eftihia, and Shaun Whishaw Brown
(1995) *Conflict resolution: A review of some non-
governmental practices*, Oxford: Refugee Studies
Programme, Queen Elizabeth House, University
of Oxford.

Williams, Suzanne (1995) *Basic Rights:
Understanding the concept and practice of basic rights
in Oxfam's programme — a resource for staff*,
unpublished mimeo, Oxford: Oxfam.